9-15-21

Book fro.
Shermon Grandy for $17.00. The transaction took place the first part of August 2021 at the Bear Cave General Store, in St. Charles Idaho. This book was written by Sherm's older brother, David Grandy.

All the
Way to
Heaven

All the Way to Heaven

Discovering God's Love in the Here and Now

DAVID GRANDY

Published by the Religious Studies Center, Brigham Young University, Provo, Utah, in cooperation with Deseret Book Company, Salt Lake City. Visit us at rsc.byu.edu. Deseret Book is a registered trademark of Deseret Book Company. Visit us at Deseret Book.com.

© 2021 by Brigham Young University. All rights reserved.

Printed in the United States of America by Sheridan Books, Inc.

Any uses of this material beyond those allowed by the exemptions in US copyright law, such as section 107, "Fair Use," and section 108, "Library Copying," require the written permission of the publisher, Religious Studies Center, 185 HGB, Brigham Young University, Provo, UT 84602. The views expressed herein are the responsibility of the authors and do not necessarily represent the position of Brigham Young University or the Religious Studies Center.

Cover and interior design by Carmen Durland Cole.

ISBN: 978-1-9503-0409-7

Library of Congress Cataloging-in-Publication Data

Names: Grandy, David, author.
Title: All the way to heaven : discovering God's love in the here and now / David Grandy.
Description: Provo, Utah : Religious Studies Center, Brigham Young University ; Salt Lake City : Deseret Book Company, [2021] | Includes index. | Summary: "The gift of mortality is an opportunity not only to prepare to meet God in the hereafter but to enjoy the gospel's glad tidings in the here and now. Scripture teaches that God's love structures the human experience and, if we are attuned to it, gives us cause to rejoice, even amid adversity. Devotion to Christ affords a wider vision of life's meaning and a foretaste of our future felicity with God. Despite necessary opposition, our mortal journey back to God can be a heavenlike experience"—Provided by publisher.
Identifiers: LCCN 2020052005 | ISBN 9781950304097 (hardcover)
Subjects: LCSH: Church of Jesus Christ of Latter-day Saints—Doctrines. | God—Love. | Mormon Church—Doctrines.
Classification: LCC BX8643.G63 G73 2021 | DDC 230/.93—dc23
LC record available at https://lccn.loc.gov/2020052005

And he said unto me: Knowest thou the condescension of God? And I said unto him: I know that he loveth his children; nevertheless, I do not know the meaning of all things.
—1 Nephi 11:16–17, The Book of Mormon: Another Testament of Jesus Christ

Eternity is in love with the productions of time.
—William Blake, *The Marriage of Heaven and Hell*

> God preaches, a noted Clergyman—
> And the sermon is never long,
> So instead of getting to Heaven, at last—
> I'm going, all along!
> —Emily Dickinson, "Some keep the Sabbath going to church"

The virtuous man delights in this world, and he delights in the next; he delights in both.
—E. A. Burtt, ed., *The Teachings of the Compassionate Buddha*

All this earthly past will have been Heaven to those who are saved.
—C. S. Lewis, *The Great Divorce*

The gospel is not a system that distrusts or despises the world. We love the earth our Heavenly Father created for us. This is the world Jesus Christ was born in as a baby, a baby who learned how to eat, sit, walk, and talk.
—Chieko N. Okazaki, *Lighten Up!*

It may even be said that the love of God already gives us, here and now, a foretaste of future felicity.
—G. W. Leibniz, "Principles of Nature and of Grace, Based on Reason"

> So he who strongly feels,
> behaves. The very bird,
> grown taller as he sings, steels
> his form straight up. Though he is captive,
> his mighty singing
> says, satisfaction is a lowly
> thing, how pure a thing is joy.
> This is mortality, this is eternity.
> —Marianne Moore, "What Are Years?"

Contents

Preface ix

Introduction xi

Chapter 1: The Long Arc of God's Love 1

Chapter 2: The Best of All Possible Worlds 21

Chapter 3: Losing Self, Finding Peace 43

Chapter 4: The Witness and Promise of Nature 59

Chapter 5: Receiving All Things with Thanksgiving 79

Index 95

About the Author 105

Preface

Although much of what follows is written in an academic register, the work is devotional. I think of it as a psalm or hymn of praise, one that reflects my imperfect understanding at the moment. Others might express similar sentiments, but they would, of course, employ different rationales and imagery. While I draw on poetry and some philosophical argument, these are meant to reinforce gospel understandings.

I am by training a philosopher, and contrary to what many may think would be the case, I have never felt religiously or spiritually threatened by philosophy. "The best thing about philosophy," explained Emmanuel Levinas, a leading ethical philosopher and religious thinker of the twentieth century, "is that it fails."[1] By failing, by never quite getting us as far as we wish, philosophy keeps us open and searching. And so also does every other endeavor that tries—initially, at least—to leave God out of the picture. We hit a wall of our own making and then must climb past it with faith that something better exists beyond it. So whatever their unique path, all people reenact Abraham's journey toward "a city . . . which hath foundations, whose builder and maker is God" (Hebrews 11:10).

This little book reflects my path. It is one of many paths, and I am sure it is marked by error. Should you run across an idea you don't like, feel free to take it with a grain of salt. The central thesis—that God's love structures our mortal experience—is what I wish to pursue, with whatever limited means are available to me. As philosopher and visual artist John F. A. Taylor remarked, "We labor after light with tools of darkness."[2]

I wish to thank two anonymous readers whose comments helped me rethink and improve parts of the text. I also thank Scott Esplin and Don Brugger of the BYU Religious Studies Center. Early in the process Scott moved things along expeditiously, and later Don and editing intern Myla Parke did a great deal to ensure the best possible outcome. I also appreciate the layout and design work of Carmen Cole and Brent Nordgren. Finally, my warmest thanks go to my wife, Janet. Her steadfast love over forty-six years informs this book on many levels.

NOTES

1. Emmanuel Levinas, interview by Richard Kearney, *Face to Face with Levinas*, ed. Richard A. Cohen (New York: SUNY Press, 1986), 22.
2. Quoted without source reference in Frank Webb, *Webb on Watercolor* (Cincinnati: North Light Books, 1990), 7.

Introduction

And we are put on earth a little space, that we may learn to bear the beams of love.
—William Blake, "The Little Black Boy"

Among Latter-day Saints it is a given that mortality is "a time to prepare to meet God" (Alma 12:24). Surely it is this, but it is also, according to Lehi, "a compound in one" wherein both the misery of hell and the happiness of heaven are on offer (2 Nephi 2:11). Trying to find the balance here, one might suggest that mortality is a state wherein we lean one way or the other, drawing from the compound a preponderance of joy or anguish. This preponderance, however, is mostly anticipatory—a foretaste adapted to the narrowness of our present understanding. As Paul wrote: "Eye hath not seen, nor ear heard, neither have entered into the heart of man, the things which God hath prepared for them that love him" (1 Corinthians 2:9). And the same is true for those who choose not to love God:

they lack the capacity to fully grasp what awaits them. We read the following description of hell in modern revelation: "The end thereof, neither the place thereof, nor their torment, no man knows; neither was it revealed, neither is, neither will be revealed unto man, except to them who are made partakers thereof; . . . wherefore, the end, the width, the height, the depth, and the misery thereof, they understand not, neither any man except those who are ordained unto this condemnation" (Doctrine and Covenants 76:45–48).

Like the man who glimpsed the beginning of infinity only to recoil from it, we cannot comprehend all that God has in store for his children. That man "sighed and stopped, shuddered and wept. His overladen heart uttered itself in tears; and he said 'Angel, I will go no farther; for the spirit of man aches with this infinity.'"[1] The mercy of God is accordingly manifest in his command that we proceed gradually—"line upon line, precept upon precept"—and thereby *grow* into his overflowing goodness. And yet there is another aspect to God's mercy that is easy to overlook, and that has to do with the earlier suggestion that the blessings of heaven are on offer in mortality. In the fourteenth century, Catherine of Siena, a Catholic patron saint and doctor of the Church, wrote, "All the way to heaven is heaven, for Jesus said, I am the Way."[2]

This statement resonates with the restored gospel in several ways, chief of which is the idea that we *progressively* make our way back to God's presence. But the surprising point of the statement is that devotion to Christ turns mortality into a heavenlike experience. This idea weaves its way through the scriptures, it seems to me, and in this little book I try to highlight some of the celestial silver linings of mortality. That is, I wish to propose that our experience

INTRODUCTION

here may be more heavenlike than we normally suppose. This, perhaps, is not a new idea; Latter-day Saints believe that much of the activity of the next world reenacts mortal experience, albeit at a higher turn of the spiral. In this book, however, I want to pick up the other end of the stick by suggesting that this world has a heavenlike structure and resonance that is often iterated out of sight through deep familiarity. This celestial resonance is (to borrow a line from T. S. Eliot) a "music heard so deeply that it is not heard at all."[3] But through attunement to gospel truths, we can begin to hear the music.

In chapter 6 of the Book of Moses we read:

> Behold, all things have their likeness, and all things are created and made to bear record of me, both things which are temporal, and things which are spiritual; things which are in the heavens above, and things which are on the earth, and things which are in the earth, and things which are under the earth, both above and beneath: all things bear record of me. (v. 63)

This venerable refrain reaches back to the Genesis narrative where God organized the various elements of creation in ways that lent meaning and understanding to human life: "Let there be lights in the firmament of the heaven to divide the day from the night; and let them be for signs, and for seasons, and for days, and years" (Genesis 1:14). Conceivably, every aspect of nature "bears record" of the Creator in some way. It is easy, generally speaking, to see the hand of God in nature's distant manifestations: "The [starry] heavens declare the glory of God," wrote the Psalmist, "and the firmament sheweth his handywork" (Psalm 19:1). To the same effect, Brigham Young remarked that of all the sciences, astronomy "gives the greatest scope to the mind."[4] In terms of physical vastness, no science can match astronomy's purview, but according to Moses, all things "on the earth" and "in the earth" and "under the earth" contribute to the celestial resonance that structures human experience. To be sure, that experience is subcelestial, but it borrows its significance from a higher sphere, much as the moon borrows light from the sun. Or so I will argue.

Consistent with Latter-day Saint thought, the idea of a heavenly way to heaven underscores the paramount significance of the here and now. We are not merely waiting for God to waft us away to a better place, but are actively working to improve our present circumstance. "Our business," said Brigham Young, "is not merely to prepare to go to another planet. This is our home."[5] Further: "This is as good an earth as need be, if we will make it so. The Lord has redeemed it, and it is his wish that his Saints should beautify it and sanctify it and bring it back to the presence of the Father and Son yet more pure, more holy and more excellent than it was in its original state, with ourselves upon it."[6]

What we do here redounds to us for good or evil, transfiguring our situation incrementally until that situation becomes our home. We grow into the heaven or hell we create on earth, and our judgment before the throne of God, according to scripture, is decided by our earthly judgment of others (see Matthew 7:1–2; Romans 2:1–5). Indeed, it seems that the commonly assumed lag time between action and consequence (whether exaltation or damnation) vanishes as our actions are reseen as the moment-to-moment judgments we visit on ourselves. John Taylor taught: "[The individual] tells the story himself, and bears witness against himself. . . . That record that is written by the man himself in the tablets of his own mind—that record that cannot lie—will in that day be unfolded before God and angels, and those

INTRODUCTION

who shall sit as judges."[7] Moreover, we come to *embody* the stories we act out: our thoughts and actions permeate and transform our being. Elder Bruce R. McConkie elaborates:

> In a real though figurative sense, the book of life is the record of the acts of men as such record is written in their own bodies. It is the record engraven on the very bones, sinews, and flesh of the mortal body. That is, every thought, word and deed has an effect on the human body; all these leave their marks, marks which can be read by Him who is Eternal as easily as the words in a book can be read. By obedience to telestial law men obtain telestial bodies; terrestrial law leads to terrestrial bodies; and conformity to celestial law—because this law includes the sanctifying power of the Holy Ghost—results in the creation of a body which is clean, pure, and spotless, a celestial body. (D&C 88:16–32.) When the book of life is opened in the day of judgment (Rev. 20:12–15), men's bodies will show what law they have lived. The Great Judge will then read the record of the book of their lives; the account of their obedience or disobedience will be written in their bodies.[8]

Alma understood that mortality is a high-stakes venture owing to the judgmental immediacy of our words, works, and thoughts (see Alma 12:14). These are the ways we decide and announce who we are, not just after the fact as we stand before God, but in the very moment we choose to obey or disobey. And if we have hardened into persons who will not repent, we have settled into a situation beyond which we cannot progress. Repentance is vital because it keeps us soft and pliant and therefore alive to the Holy Ghost, whose impressions gently reshape us into celestial beings. Without those impressions—without that outside help—we would all plateau at a subcelestial level.

Not only that, but those impressions are "happifying," to use a word long fallen out of Latter-day Saint circulation. They enable us to live "after the manner of happiness" (2 Nephi 5:27), which is very different from "living happily ever after." The latter refrain sums up the conventional view of happiness, which is one of Satan's great half-truths: carefree placidity. The former rounds out the latter by allowing us to realize that life is a "compound in one" wherein carefree placidity is meaningful only as it is balanced against challenge and turmoil. And so—and this is part of the gospel miracle—happiness may reign amid placidity, turbulence, and even pain. But only as God's unfathomable love begins to swell our hearts. In the words of a hymn familiar to Latter-day Saints:

> I stand all amazed at the love Jesus offers me,
> Confused at the grace that so fully he proffers me.
> I tremble to know that for me he was crucified,
> That for me, a sinner, he suffered, he bled and died.[9]

Happiness and pain can comingle, particularly as we feel the depth of the Savior's sacrificial love and through our own sufferings win fellowship with Christ. This is a thread that runs through the New Testament epistles: Christians do not suffer just to suffer, but in a world where pain is inevitable, they may tap into the power of the Atonement by assimilating their own hardships to those of Christ, who, after all, freely underwent far greater humiliations on our behalf. For his sake, wrote Paul, "I have suffered the loss of all things, and do count them but dung, that I may win Christ, . . . that I may know him, and the power of his resurrection, and the *fellowship of his sufferings*, being made conformable unto his death; if by any means I might attain

INTRODUCTION

unto the resurrection of the dead" (Philippians 3:8, 10–11; emphasis added).

For Paul, happiness sprang into existence with Christ's victory over death, and if Christ had not achieved that victory, we would be "of all men most miserable" (1 Corinthians 15:19). Paul accordingly deemed it a small sacrifice—or perhaps no sacrifice at all—to "suffer the loss of all things" in order to become like Christ. He also learned that the glad message of the gospel makes one glad *in this life*. It is at once a promissory note of "the unsearchable riches" of God's grace and a gift that enables one to experience the "peace of God, which passeth all understanding" in this world (Ephesians 3:8; Philippians 4:7). That peace, he wrote, caused him to rejoice; further, it afforded him spiritual and emotional equilibrium as he passed through the ups and downs of everyday life: "For I have learned, in whatsoever state I am, therewith to be content. I know both how to be abased, and I know how to abound: every where and in all things I am instructed both to be full and to be hungry, both to abound and to suffer need" (Philippians 4:11–12).

Obviously Paul is unusual in his devotion to Christ. He felt his personal failings keenly as he preached the gospel and consequently tried to rely wholly on Christ, believing that such reliance would make up the difference between his faltering presentation and the splendor of his message. Only in this way, he said, could God's majesty be displayed—as it rested on the weak disciple of Christ and thereby allowed others to sense firsthand the rescuing power of a loving God (see 1 Corinthians 2:1–5). Though Paul may be unusual in his devotion to Christ—or at least unusual in the way he expresses that devotion—he falls squarely among prophets and apostles of every dispensation who have declared the gospel message. That message is happifying because the benefits of living the gospel vastly outweigh the costs. Indeed, the costs may be said to be seed crystals of benefits yet unrealized, according to Brigham Young, because they gradually turn to our good and thereby fit us for the kingdom of heaven. After rehearsing the early tribulations of the Latter-day Saints, he stated: "Where, then, is the sacrifice this people have ever made? There is no such thing—they have only exchanged a worse condition for a better one, every time they have been moved—they have exchanged ignorance for knowledge, and inexperience for its opposite."[10]

It is easy, of course, to speak this way from the pulpit, particularly when one is not passing through a heavy trial. Better generally to extend sympathy to those who suffer than to pontificate from the podium—or one's writing desk—about the long-range benefits of hardship. But the gospel message runs deep, and its gladness does not attenuate as troubles mount. Indeed, that is when the saving power of the gospel manifests itself most richly. "Where danger is," wrote the great German lyric poet and philosopher Friedrich Hölderlin, "also grows the saving power."[11] We are saved amid extremity, and sometimes we have to be reminded by the hard knocks of life that our present situation is fleeting and tenuous. Those hard knocks pull us down into the oceanic depths of Christ's Atonement, for otherwise we are inclined to sail on its surface, taking our personal blessings for granted because "the breadth, and length, and depth, and height" of God's love have never really occurred to us (see Ephesians 3:18–19). In this state of mind we tend to associate happiness with the raft we are sailing on—and with the goods we have thereon amassed—and not with the vast ocean that makes the sailing experience possible in the first place. Not that this outlook is wrong, but it is, by my reading of the scriptures, limited. If the gospel is to make us *unconditionally* glad, there must be something absolutely universal to celebrate—a gift all people know, regardless of individual circumstances, talents, and possessions. This is, as Brigham Young said, the opportunity to be here and gain experience;[12] or, as Paul put it, to "live, and move, and have our being" (Acts 17:28). I think of it as being kept afloat by God's love while learning to sail on our own.

Without that love we would be permanently grounded and absolutely miserable. We would be, in Lehi's words, "devils, angels to a devil" (2 Nephi 9:9). So the glad message of the gospel is much more than just good news of the everyday variety. It subsists in the realization that mortal experience is not a given but a priceless gift. Whatever our setbacks and hardships, we can yet rejoice in the opportunity to be challenged and knocked about for some purpose beyond our mortal imagining. Recall James's words: "My brethren, count it all joy when ye fall into divers temptations [trials]; knowing this, that the trying of your faith worketh patience. But let patience have her perfect work, that ye may be perfect and entire, wanting nothing" (James 1:2–4). Going further, Sister Chieko N. Okazaki, while serving as first counselor in the Relief Society General Presidency, wrote that gratitude should also be thrown into the mix: "When we thank God for our trials, tribulations, irritations, and afflictions, something happens to transform them into blessings."[13]

When Sister Okazaki and James admonish us to find joy in hardship, they are measuring their happiness from the bottom up, just as Catherine of Siena, Paul, and Brigham Young did and as other followers of Christ choose to do. Yet the normal tendency is to measure happiness from the top down, noting the things we lack while overlooking the blessings we habitually enjoy and that from moment to moment prop us up. Such top-down reckoning engenders dissatisfaction, envy, self-loathing, and even anger. Upon grasping the wider vision the gospel offers, however, we realize that long before our "lack" came to control our thinking, we were blessed beyond measure by Christ's willing sacrifice on our behalf. What we already have, and have as a free gift, is incomparably more than what we lack. Not only that, but the little we lack may be the means whereby we learn to love others, who also wrestle with their own lack.

My goal in writing this book is to try to see to the bottom of God's love. I will, of course, fail in this endeavor because of my weakness and, more significantly, because there is no bottom. But there is value in the effort. We are accustomed to believe that God's blessings begin with good health, financial stability, professional success, and so on. Starting the tally so late in the game, however, spawns frustration and dissatisfaction when these blessings go unrealized. And then when some are realized, we may feel that God has finally—after a season of sacrifice and want—opened the windows of heaven. To be sure, he has done just that, but, truth be told, his most significant blessings were in place long before we turned to him for help. Those blessings are the ones Catherine of Siena had in mind when she remarked that "all the way to heaven is heaven." Our mere arrival here, when seen against the wide canvas of God's plan of happiness, is cause for celebration. What is more, mortality, while not heaven, is a kind of "Easter in ordinary,"[14] a fallen world resonant with heavenly love. That, too, is reason to rejoice.

INTRODUCTION

NOTES

1. John Paul Richter, "Dream Vision of the Infinite," cited in James E. Talmage, "The Earth and Man," http://ndbf.blogspot.com/2006/08/.
2. Quoted in Kelly S. Johnson, *The Fear of Beggars: Stewardship and Poverty in Christian Ethics* (Grand Rapids, MI: Eerdmans, 2007), 209.
3. T. S. Eliot, "The Dry Salvages," in *T. S. Eliot: The Complete Poems and Plays: 1909–1950* (New York: Harcourt, Brace, and World, 1952), 136.
4. Brigham Young, in *Journal of Discourses*, 26 vols. (London: Latter-day Saints' Book Depot, 1854–86), 7:2.
5. Brigham Young, in *Journal of Discourses*, 8:297.
6. Brigham Young, in *Journal of Discourses*, 10:177.
7. John Taylor, in *Journal of Discourses*, 11:79.
8. Bruce R. McConkie, *Mormon Doctrine*, 2nd ed. (Salt Lake City: Bookcraft, 1979), 97.
9. "I Stand All Amazed," *Hymns of The Church of Jesus Christ of Latter-day Saints*, rev. ed. (Salt Lake City: The Church of Jesus Christ of Latter-day Saints, 2002), no. 193.
10. Brigham Young, in *Journal of Discourses*, 1:314.
11. From the opening lines of his 1803 poem "Patmos," English translation at https://www.poemhunter.com/poem/patmos/.
12. Brigham Young, in *Journal of Discourses*, 7:333.
13. Chieko N. Okazaki, *Lighten Up!* (Salt Lake City: Deseret Book, 1993), 45.
14. I take this phrase from Nicholas Lash's fine book *Easter in Ordinary: Reflections on Human Experience and the Knowledge of God* (Charlottesville, VA: University of Virginia Press, 1988).

CHAPTER 1

The Long Arc of God's Love

For I am persuaded, that neither death, nor life, nor angels, nor principalities, nor powers, nor things present, nor things to come, nor height, nor depth, nor any other creature, shall be able to separate us from the love of God, which is in Christ Jesus our Lord.
        —the Apostle Paul, Epistle to the Romans 8:38–39

In the process of breaking the frame of everyday experience, the gospel restores and makes real the forgotten possibilities of youth. Henry David Thoreau wrote, "The youth gets together his materials to build a bridge to the moon, or, perchance, a palace or temple on the earth, and, at length, the middle-aged man concludes to build a woodshed with them."[1] Mortality has a way of deflating our dreams and trimming us down to size. This, of course, is not all bad—to be successful in life we need to know our weaknesses as well as our strengths. But for many, early childhood is a time of boundless optimism, and it is as if we arrived here from a better, more promising sphere. Recall

ALL THE WAY TO HEAVEN

William Wordsworth's recollection of early youth:

> There was a time when meadow, grove, and stream,
> The earth, and every common sight,
> To me did seem
> Apparell'd in celestial light,
> The glory and the freshness of a dream.[2]

Later in the ode, Wordsworth ventures that the celestial light that suffuses our youthful apprehension of nature arises from our heavenly home:

> Our birth is but a sleep and a forgetting:
> The Soul that rises with us, our life's Star,
> Hath had elsewhere its setting,
> And cometh from afar:
> Not in entire forgetfulness,
> And not in utter nakedness,
> But trailing clouds of glory do we come
> From God, who is our home.

In other words (and this is Wordsworth's next line): "Heaven lies about us in our infancy!"

These lines are well known to Latter-day Saints because they affirm our belief in a pre-earth life. Some also believe that while memories of that life may briefly linger after birth, they eventually fade into what Wordsworth called "the light of common day." The present world closes in on us and commandeers our thinking, inclining us toward fully naturalistic understandings of ourselves and the situation that, it may seem, we just happened to chance upon. Not sure of how we got here, or why we might be here, we cannot be sure of what comes next. But God has given us the gospel, which is a lens through which we see the world with eyes of faith and by which we recapture the bright and buoyant optimism of childhood.

OPTIMISM REGAINED AND BIG-PICTURE UNDERSTANDING

A case in point is the conversion of F. Enzio Busche and his family. As a young teenager Enzio was drafted into the German army during the last year of World War II. Like many others, he suffered incredible hardship after the war while Germany was rebuilding its infrastructure and economy. He eventually finished high school, studied at the university level, and took over his family's printing business. Married in 1955, he and his wife Jutta began their family. By this time he was a successful businessman. Then in 1958 two Latter-day Saint missionaries knocked on his door. As an emeritus member of the Seventy many years later, Elder Busche related his family's conversion, comparing it to his childhood Christmas experience.[3] On the day of Christmas Eve the adults would send the children out to play and spend the day cleaning and decorating the house. When the house was spick-and-span, generally in the late afternoon, they would bring in the children, bathe them, and dress them in their best clothes. Then they would gather them together and bring them into a living room that was radiant with candles and Christmas lights. For Enzio it was like being taken to another world. The Christmas experience was good and clean and wholesome. It was spiritual.

Enzio stated that as he grew older he decided that the spiritual aspect of Christmas wasn't real. It was too good to be true, just a childhood experience that one had to outgrow in order to get on with the real business of life—going to school, getting a job, and achieving wealth and success. So he followed this path until those two missionaries knocked on his door and he was impressed to invite them in. Getting to know them and hearing their message, he recalled, was like rediscovering Christmas: "There was something in these missionaries—a glow of trust, a glow of hope, a glow of security, and a glow of love—that looked in the beginning to us like a fairy tale." They had a spiritual radiance about them, and as a consequence Enzio and his family joined the Church. What he had written off as fanciful and too good to be true became real to him again, but this time in a deeper, truer way. In 1977 Enzio became a General Authority of the Church when he was called to the First Quorum of the Seventy.

Along with renewing our childlike faith and optimism, the restored gospel, Elder Boyd K. Packer taught, gives us the big picture, which resembles a three-act play.[4] The first act sets the stage for mortality, and without the knowledge of what occurred in premortality, it is impossible to make complete sense of the second act, which begins with our physical birth. Not only that, but it is impossible to fully grasp the scope of God's love. Not knowing what happened before our arrival on earth, we are almost sure to overlook the ways God's blessings tumble into this world from an earlier world. First of all, by pushing back the gospel narrative to that earlier world, the restored gospel heightens our appreciation of the Savior's sacrifice on our behalf. Christ was, as John said, "the Lamb slain from the foundation of the world" (Revelation 13:8). Something momentous happened early on, something that thereafter lends lasting significance to the events that play out in mortality. This something, Latter-day Saints believe, is the premortal Christ's willing assent to suffer on behalf of all people so that they might, on condition of repentance, return to live with God at a higher turn of the gospel spiral. After our mortal sojourn, Christ's Atonement allows us to return to God enriched by our away-from-home experiences but no longer tainted by them.

The Book of Mormon is instructive in this regard. Although it has little to say about premortality, it nevertheless stretches us beyond the mortal horizons of birth and death. In my opinion the first great moment in the Book of Mormon occurs when Nephi prays to make larger sense of things. His two older brothers are rebelling against their father Lehi, who has, for reasons they cannot fathom, left Jerusalem and taken his family into the wilderness. In retrospect we know that Nephi was right to support his father, but at the time he could not have known—at least, initially—that God was leading Lehi into the long sweep of sacred history. It took prayer to introduce Nephi to that possibility, and even then he came away with no details but just the assurance that he should follow his father. Here is what he says about the experience:

> And it came to pass that I, Nephi, being exceedingly young, nevertheless being large in stature, and also having great desires to know of the mysteries of God, wherefore, I did cry unto the Lord; and behold he did visit me, and did soften my heart that I did believe all the words which had been spoken by my father; wherefore, I did not rebel against him like unto my brothers. (1 Nephi 2:16)

Later, Nephi will begin to develop a big-picture understanding of why the Lord has led his family into the wilderness: it was not just to escape the Babylonian destruction of Jerusalem, but also to plant a saving branch or remnant of Israel in a remote part of God's vineyard. As this understanding dawns on Nephi, he finds solace in the writings of Isaiah, who prophesied that though God would scatter his ancient covenant people, he would never forget them and would, at last, joyfully and redemptively gather them together again. For those on the front end of this many-century, multigenerational endeavor, though, things might have seemed dreary at times. Nephi's brother Jacob, who like Nephi surely felt connected to Jerusalem by reason of his Old World birth, also quoted Isaiah, no doubt in part as healing balm. In his closing words, however, Jacob seems unable to mask the hurt that lingers for those cut off from their ancestral home:

> And it came to pass that I, Jacob, began to be old; and the record of this people being kept on the other plates of Nephi, wherefore, I conclude this record, declaring that I have written according to the best of my knowledge, by saying that the time passed away with us, and also our lives passed away like as it were unto us a dream, we being a lonesome and a solemn people, wanderers, cast out from Jerusalem, born in tribulation, in a wilderness, and hated of our brethren, which caused wars and contentions; wherefore, we did mourn out our days. (Jacob 7:26)

The mournful beauty of the passage echoes the following lines from Psalm 137, which express the gloom of Jews forcibly driven out of Jerusalem by their Babylonian captors.

> By the rivers of Babylon there we sat down, yea, we wept, when we remembered Zion. We hanged our harps upon the willows in the midst thereof. For there they that carried us away captive required of us a song; and they that wasted us required of us mirth, saying, Sing us one of the songs of Zion. How shall we sing the Lord's song in a strange land?

THE LONG ARC OF GOD'S LOVE

> If I forget thee, O Jerusalem, let my right hand forget her cunning. If I do not remember thee, let my tongue cleave to the roof of my mouth; if I prefer not Jerusalem above my chief joy. (Psalm 137:1–6)

Along with Jacob and Nephi, the Psalmist feels the tug of Jerusalem—its sacred environs and ancestral memories. But thanks to earlier prophets (particularly Isaiah), all three have reason to believe that a larger story is now in progress, one that spans generations and far-flung geographic barriers. In the Bible we learn of Israelites driven into Assyria and then, a century later, into Babylon. Both of these forced migrations were not without sacred rhyme or reason, according to Isaiah, for in God's own time he will gather together those whom he has scattered. This is the prospect that comforts Nephi and Jacob, whose family is projected far beyond Assyria and Babylon.

Sometimes challenges are quickly overcome, sometimes not. As Lehi's family journeys through the Old World wilderness of the Arabian Peninsula, Laman and Lemuel continue their rebellion, hoping to reverse the migration and return to Jerusalem. As months turn into years, perhaps they resign themselves to dying in the wilderness or, much better, in the land Bountiful at the edge of the Indian Ocean. In any event, they never see their hardship as the first chapter of a long, multigenerational story whose far-distant ending completes God's grand purpose of saving his children. Nephi, however, by remaining open to the impressions of the Holy Ghost, is prophetically schooled to think and feel more vastly, which is why he states in his closing words that he "pray[s] the Father in the name of Christ that many of us, if not all, may be saved in his kingdom at that great and last day" (2 Nephi 33:12).

"Many of us, if not all." Were it not for the narrative in which it is embedded, this phrase might be taken as empty rhetoric, an idiom easy to mouth but hard to feel. But Nephi's story, as he relates it, suggests a gradual acclimation to divine thought, and no doubt his experiences caused his heart to swell "wide as eternity," as it was said of Enoch (Moses 7:41). There is, after all, the heartbreak entailed by ongoing disharmony within his family, a breach that will widen once they reach the New World. What is more, he learns by revelation of the degeneracy, conquest, and apostasy of his posterity many generations hence (see 1 Nephi 12:19–23). So while Nephi is lifted up to the Lord in vision and given expansive understanding, he often feels weighed down by that understanding, entailing as it does a knowledge of his posterity's disobedience and misery.

For example, after Nephi sees in vision the destruction of his seed, he returns to his father's tent to find his wayward brothers disputing Lehi's prophetic claims. At first Nephi cannot engage them; he is too drained and demoralized by what he has just seen in vision, the dark prospect of which is unfolding right before him:

> And now I, Nephi, was grieved because of the hardness of their hearts, and also, because of the things which I had seen, and knew they must unavoidably come to pass because of the great wickedness of the children of men. And it came to pass that I was overcome because of my afflictions, for I considered that mine afflictions were great above all, because of the destruction of my people, for I had beheld their fall. (1 Nephi 15:4–5)

Gradually, however, he is able to gather strength to ask a simple question: "Have ye inquired of the Lord?" (1 Nephi 15:8). Since prayer was the point at which Nephi's path diverged from that of his brothers, he admonishes them to take this first step toward big-picture understanding. They, however, respond: "We have not [inquired of the Lord]; for the Lord maketh no such thing known unto us" (v. 9). Careful to protect their position vis à vis their younger brother, they launch an oddly reasoned preemptive strike against the very possibility of divine revelation. Determined not to pray, they insist that God will not answer their prayers.

Laman and Lemuel's myopia is self-inflicted. By remaining narcissistically attached to their own personal hardships, they never glimpse the larger pattern of things that would turn those hardships into priceless blessings. For all their failings, however, Laman and Lemuel are not evil in an over-the-top way. They are recognizably human. If my observations may be trusted, many of us who profess belief in God kick against (or would kick against) the kind of wholesale disruptive change that uprooted Lehi's family. In the moment that tribulation unexpectedly overtakes us, we, like Laman and Lemuel, find it hard to get long-range perspective on things. We do not have the distance that history naturally supplies, nor the advantage of viewing our experience through some yet-to-be-written sacred record. Lacking these same helps, Laman and Lemuel behave as fairly normal human beings; they are instances of what King Benjamin called the "natural man" (Mosiah 3:19), and they struggle to make sense of what strikes them as a senseless situation. Nephi, however, is dramatically different; he does not fall within the range of everyday human behavior, owing to his prayerful reliance on the Lord.

UNDERSTANDING NEPHI

To gain some appreciation of Nephi's goodness and the book he inaugurates (the Book of Mormon), consider the following. Again, if my experience may be trusted as representative of Latter-day Saint devotion, it is safe to say that all faithful members of the Church want to go to heaven, and they worry in that regard about their children, grandchildren, friends, and neighbors. But Nephi, as noted, is concerned about "all of God's children," not as a way of adding to his prayer a nice rhetorical flourish, but because he has caught sight of the long arc of God's love as it spans generations and geographic barriers.

We partially catch sight of that arc. Our hearts are stretched or turned back toward our ancestors and forward toward our posterity, but rarely (it seems to me) for more than a few generations in either direction. At some point things grow dim, owing to our inability to imagine real, living people from nothing more than a birthdate, say, or, in the case of distant posterity, from nothing more than the prospect of a birthdate. But Nephi sees much more, which is why the Book of Mormon is a book of prophetic horizons. He sees in advance much of the thousand-year sweep of the book, but his vision does not stop there. He sees our day as well. What makes his vision compelling is that he is not concerned with historical events per se; he is concerned with family and multigenerational familial happiness.

Which is to say Nephi's yardstick for taking the measure of history is very different from the modern yardstick. Because he does not reflexively assume that history has been a Stone Age to Information Age ascent out of an abyss of ignorance, he does not try to track that ascent in terms of science, technology, economic policy, and so on. These endeavors may ease (and complicate) the human condition, but they do not of themselves empower a society to live "after the manner of happiness" (2 Nephi 5:27). Obedience to gospel principles does this, and such obedience (unlike manned spaceflight or the latest cell phone technology, say) is within the reach of all people who have been gathered into the Abrahamic covenant, irrespective of place or time. Given this understanding, Nephi can readily grasp why his family is being scattered beyond Jerusalem: God wishes to leaven the loaf of humanity with the saving power of the Abrahamic covenant.

This alone is what counts as history for Nephi—God's saving work, his endeavor to rescue many, if not all, of his children. And because this work involves the mingling of Israel into non-Israel (the intergrafting of tame and wild olive branches for the betterment of both), it is a work that cannot begin and end in a single lifetime or even several lifetimes. While for most believers the clock starts ticking at birth, quits ticking at death, and then some sort of summative judgment is made of one's life, Nephi has been caught up to the higher perspective of multigenerational rise and fall, and he feels his own life is significant to the degree that it lifts others heavenward—whether those in his immediate family or, just as importantly and no less real, those to be born in the distant future.

For Nephi there is hope for everyone, for in God's plan "time and tide flow wide."[5] If he could speak to us today, he would insist that the saving work of God entails far-flung family interconnections that overcome the separating effects of space and time and thereby explode the modern conceit that "I am my own person." Where most of us see distance and separation as we look down the corridor of the centuries, Nephi sees continuity and even unity. Where we see single-handed, single-generation, or several-generation accomplishment (e.g., the "Greatest Generation," the Industrial Revolution), he sees many-handed, multigenerational rise and fall. To be sure, he believes individuals may act on their own, but often they are swept along by tradition. Even when they believe they are free of the past, they resonate to and mediate the good and the bad of their ancestors. For Nephi, then, history is more participatory, more tightly interwoven across the centuries, and more dependent on long-reverberating acts of obedience and disobedience than most people now suppose. That is why he likens scriptural narrative to his own experience—he wants us to know that there are no spectators to the Book of Mormon (see 1 Nephi 19:23). We, like Nephi, are part of that story, though we are *latter-day* participants in a salvation drama that reaches back to the saving promises made to Old Testament patriarchs.

AT THE OTHER END OF THE BOOK OF MORMON—MORONI AND HIS PROMISE

If the youthful Nephi's prayer is the moment that led him into what Paul called "the breadth, and length, and depth, and height" of God's love (Ephesians 3:18), Moroni's closing promise reenacts that moment by asking readers to reflect on God's long-suffering love as it expresses itself in the Book of Mormon narrative—and, what is more, as that love has now miraculously overleapt the time frame of the record itself and materialized as a book through which the voice of an ancient people "crying from the dust" may be heard (2 Nephi 33:13). I confess that I missed this point for many years.

As a young missionary, I directed investigators to Moroni 10:4–5.

> And when ye shall receive these things, I would exhort you that ye would ask God, the Eternal Father, in the name of Christ, if these things are not true; and if ye shall ask with a sincere heart, with real intent, having faith in Christ, he will manifest the truth of it unto you, by the power of the Holy Ghost. And by the power of the Holy Ghost ye may know the truth of all things.

While I did not doubt the veracity of the promise, I did note that most people we taught did not receive a witness of the Book of Mormon, even though many claimed to have prayed with a "sincere heart" and "real intent." That was a bit puzzling to me. Decades later, however, I read Moroni 10:3 and realized that, like Nephi, Moroni feels that once readers grasp how merciful God has been toward all his children, they will begin to realize or "remember" how merciful he has been to each person—each reader—individually. <u>In some manner hard to comprehend, God's universal love distills upon each person individually.</u>

> Behold, I would exhort you that when ye shall read these things, if it be wisdom in God that ye should read them, that ye would remember how merciful the Lord hath been unto the children of men, from the creation of Adam even down until the time that ye shall receive these things, and ponder it in your hearts.

The word *remember* is particularly interesting in this verse. How can someone who has never read the Book of Mormon, or perhaps any Christian scripture whatsoever, "remember" God's loving-kindness to his children "from the creation of Adam" down unto the present moment?

They cannot, of course, until they begin to prayerfully read holy scripture and experience the impressions of the Holy Ghost, which "bring[s] all things to [one's] remembrance" (John 14:26). The word of God, prayerfully received, opens the mind to larger possibilities, some of which recapture the forgotten hopes of childhood, just as Elder Busche experienced. And certainly, by stretching us upward toward God and outward toward our fellowmen, prayerful immersion in holy writ allows us to realize our commonality with others. No matter how different others may seem, and no matter the time and place of their mortal state, we share with them the same earthbound predicament, the same vulnerability to sickness, hurt, and death; and given that vulnerability (what the scriptures call our fallen nature), we may all rejoice in the gospel realization that a loving God has provided an escape therefrom. But first we must follow Nephi and Moroni as they teach us to pray.

The primordial intrigue of prayer is that it attunes us to a larger resonance of things, enabling our entry (or reentry) into moments of expansive jubilation, the like of which attended the birth of Jesus: "And suddenly there was with the angel a multitude of the heavenly host praising God, and saying, Glory to God in the highest, and on earth peace, good will toward men" (Luke 2:13–14). The restored gospel helps us to know that this jubilation reaches back to the premortal existence, where "the morning stars sang together, and the sons [and daughters] of God shouted for joy" (Job 38:7) when the premortal Jehovah offered himself as a sacrificial lamb in order to bring about God's plan to save "many, if not all," of his children. Of this momentous event, Latter-day Saint scholar Hugh Nibley observed that "when the plan was announced to the assembled hosts, and the full scope and magnanimity of it dawned upon them, they burst into spontaneous shouts of joy and joined in a hymn of praise and thanksgiving, the morning song of Creation, which remains to this day the archetype of hymns, the great *acclamatio*, the primordial nucleus of all liturgy."[6]

John the Revelator numbered the participants in this great choir as "ten thousand times ten thousand, and thousands of thousands" (Revelation 5:11). We participate in it every time we bear witness of God's goodness in word or deed; we evoke the great hymn, tap into its cosmic resonance, and feel it echoing in our soul, according to Elder Jeffrey R. Holland. "There are several reasons for bearing testimony," he stated while speaking to the missionaries of the Church: "One is that when you declare the truth, it will bring an echo, a memory, even if it is an unconscious, memory to the investigator, that they have heard this truth before—and of course they have. A missionary's testimony invokes a great legacy of testimony dating back to the councils in heaven before this world was. There, in an earlier place, these same people heard this same plan outlined and heard there the role that Jesus Christ would play in their salvation."[7]

The great hymn may be said to restate the Word of creation, which "was in the beginning with God" and whereby "all things were made" and without which "was not anything made that was made" (John 1:1–3).[8] The Atonement being its keynote, it celebrates the unfathomable love of God, which love "descend[s] below all things" and thereby brings all things together—harmoniously, cosmically (Doctrine and Covenants 88:6; 122:8). The Apostle Paul made this point when he insisted that by virtue of Christ's atoning sacrifice "all things" are brought before God and thereby "hold together," whether "things on earth or things in heaven" (Colossians 1:15–20, New International Version).

This deep mutuality and reconciliation of difference—this *at-one-ment*—brings things together, just as the harmonic assimilation of different musical tones produces a single hymn. Although each tone is distinctive, each plays off the others (each is reconciled to the others) so that the deeply satisfying outcome is a single musical composition rather than a disjointed succession of sounds.

At the level of the individual believer, the promise of God is that gospel obedience brings the different parts of our lives into harmony so that even our "wilderness" years, our seasons of hardship and disappointment, are retroactively charged with significance. Nothing is lost in God's economy; nothing is senseless. Every valiant effort, no matter how disappointing the immediate result, will be redeemed, will be repackaged into a larger pattern of meaning and given back to us as a gift. "I will restore to you the years that the locust hath eaten, the cankerworm, and the caterpiller, and the palmerworm, my great army which I sent among you," the Lord promises in the book of Joel. "And ye shall eat in plenty, and be satisfied, and praise the name of the Lord your God, that hath dealt wondrously with you: and my people shall never be ashamed" (Joel 2:25–26).

This wondrous work unfolds on many levels as the saving, reconciling power of Christ's Atonement "descends below all things"—below all hatred, all strife, all declaration of absolute enmity and apartness—to heal from within and to bring us into remembrance of events older and more foundational than the daily triumphs, hurts, and hostilities that routinely monopolize our interest. When Moroni admonishes us to "remember how merciful the Lord hath been unto the children of men, from the creation of Adam even down until the time that ye shall receive these things," he has every reason, it would seem, *not* to remember God's mercy. From the limited perspective of the present moment, his cause is lost: he is in the middle of a bloodbath, an everyday witness to spiritual depravity and physical atrocity, and because the mad frenzy is irreversible, his only recourse is to ride the tide of events while hiding from those who wish to kill him. Where is God in all this? Where is his mercy? From the point of view of those in the middle of the slaughter, nowhere, it would seem. Remarkably, however, Moroni does not despair, even as the slaughter rages and threatens to destroy him. Like Nephi, he has perceived the long arc of God's love as it stretches beyond the horizons of mortal experience, and his principal concern is to plant the seed of faith in the hearts of people yet unborn.

We, of course, are among those people, and the Book of Mormon is that seed. To vary the metaphor, the Book of Mormon is an integral part of God's long rhyme of salvation. Though its narrative begins with family discord and ends with the chaotic destruction of a once-happy people, the book itself ends on a promising, uplifting note. Moroni, after all, knows that there is a bigger story in the offing, and he trusts that God can find a rhyme where most humans find nothing but chaotic finality and senseless, irredeemable ruin. But, again, the difference is that Moroni has tasted of God's redemptive love through prayer, and he thus knows that God is merciful beyond mortal imagining. God's work of salvation unfolds across millennia, and it involves the mutual uplift of all people as cultures intermix and the living and dead reach out to each other in the temple.

This is the wondrous mercy of God that, when remembered, melts or softens hearts. It is what William Shakespeare called "sweet love remembered," and he described its transforming power in his twenty-ninth sonnet. Although the sonnet is not explicitly religious, it does track the process of prayer—the struggle to break out of one's narcissistic cocoon into the free air of God's love.

> When, in disgrace with fortune and men's eyes,
> I all alone beweep my outcast state,
> And trouble deaf heaven with my bootless cries,
> And look upon myself and curse my fate,
> Wishing me like to one more rich in hope,
> Featur'd like him, like him with friends possess'd,
> Desiring this man's art and that man's scope,
> With what I most enjoy contented least;
> Yet in these thoughts myself almost despising,
> Haply I think on thee, and then my state,
> Like to the lark at break of day arising
> From sullen earth, sings hymns at heaven's gate;
> For thy sweet love rememb'red such wealth brings
> That then I scorn to change my state with kings.[9]

While it makes sense to suppose, as many scholars do, that Shakespeare's sweet remembered love is a close friend, the mention of daybreak and of the lark singing "hymns at heaven's gate" catalyzes the sonnet's sudden spiritual expansion and imbues the last lines with the suggestion of otherworldly rescue. That suggestion, I propose, is Shakespeare's way of skirmishing with the wondrous truth of a loving God who unfailingly and everlastingly remembers his children and who asks in return that they remember him. The invitation to remember is meant primarily to fulfill our need for the expansive joy that prayerful remembrance brings, not God's need for praise—though we will thank and praise God and even jubilate once the revelation of his long-enduring, long-continuing love begins to register.

"Herein is love," wrote John, "not that we loved God, but that he loved us, and sent his Son to be the propitiation for our sins" (1 John 4:10). And, a few verses later: "We love him, because he first loved us" (v. 19). God took the first step, thereby obliging reciprocity on our part. But according to John, God's gift of love was so magnanimous that nothing less than Christlike love can be offered to God in return. God's love is its own medium of exchange, and when we are filled with it, we freely love others as God has loved us. Like Nephi and Moroni, we are stretched out toward others along the long arc of God's love, and in that holier state we are rescued from the particularity of our own mortal circumstance and the narcissistic tendency to save only ourselves.

NOTES

1. Henry David Thoreau, *The Heart of Thoreau's Journals*, ed. Odell Shepard (New York: Dover, 1961), 94.
2. William Wordsworth, "Ode: Intimations of Immortality from Recollections of Early Childhood," in *Oxford Book of English Verse, 1250–1900*, ed. Arthur Quiller-Couch (Oxford: Clarendon Press, 1912), 608.
3. Enzio Busche, "Christmas Every Day," *Liahona*, December 2001.
4. Boyd K. Packer, "The Great Plan of Happiness," https://www.churchofjesuschrist.org/manual/book-of-mormon-teacher-resource-manual/appendix/the-great-plan-of-happiness.
5. Herman Melville, *Moby-Dick* (New York: Norton, 1967), 148.
6. Hugh W. Nibley, "Treasures in the Heavens," *Nibley on the Timely and the Timeless* (Salt Lake City: Publishers Press, 1978), 51.
7. Jeffrey R. Holland, "Missionary Work and the Atonement," *Ensign*, March 2001.
8. While John's identification of Christ with the Word (*logos*) obviously refers to Christ's role in the creation of the world, it also may be said to reach back to the role Christ played in the Council in Heaven. We read in the book of Revelation that during the War in Heaven, Lucifer launched a war of words—he accused his brethren "before . . . God day and night"; those who opposed him,

however, were able to "overcome him by the blood of the Lamb, and by the word of their testimony" (Revelation 12:7–11).
9. William Shakespeare, Sonnet 29, in *The Complete Works of Shakespeare*, 3rd ed., ed. David Bevington (Glenview, IL: Scott, Foresman and Company, 1980), 1588.

CHAPTER 2

The Best of All Possible Worlds

> *By the mediation of a thousand little mosses and fungi the most unsightly objects become radiant with beauty. . . . For seen with the eye of a poet, as God sees them, all things are alive and beautiful.*
> —Henry David Thoreau, *Early Spring in Massachusetts*

I proposed in the last chapter that God's love, his care for us, stretches out of sight in both directions, back before our birth and far into the future after our death. That love, I might add, is synonymous with his saving work, which, according to scripture, is bound up not merely with the rise and fall of civilizations but also with the coming and going of worlds:

> The Lord God spake unto Moses, saying: The heavens, they are many, and they cannot be numbered unto man; but they are numbered unto me, for they are mine. And as one earth shall pass away, and the heavens thereof even so shall another come; and there is no end to my works, neither to my words. For behold, this is my work and my

glory—to bring to pass the immortality and eternal life of man. (Moses 1:37–39)

Amid this coming and going of worlds, God's eye lights upon each individual and providentially guides him or her along a path that redounds to the happiness and exaltation of all people. Thus the long arc of God's love also entails the care with which God threads each life into the vast tapestry of cosmic history, a small stretch of which is our earthbound passage through mortality.

As the scripture just cited indicates, the restored gospel assigns value to the physical universe: as worlds roll into and out of existence, God performs the long miracle of his saving work. His love, one might venture, is astronomical, both in the sense that the cosmos is his sphere of action ("Behold, all these [astronomical bodies] are kingdoms, and any man who hath seen any or the least of these hath seen God moving in his majesty and power," Doctrine and Covenants 88:47) and in the sense that his patience exceeds the familiar temporal reckonings of mortality. "God sees the truth, but waits," wrote the great Russian novelist Leo Tolstoy.[1] Seeing the truth of who we can be, our celestial potential, God situates us in spiritually promising circumstances and then patiently waits for us to repent. Given the profound disparity between our mortal frailty and our Abrahamic longing for a "city . . . whose builder and maker is God" (Hebrews 11:10), the journey to be traveled may require a setting no less vast than the physical universe, the spatial and temporal bounds of which stagger the mortal imagination. Indeed, the immensity of the universe, when viewed naturalistically, is often seen as evidence of human insignificance: we are so tiny and short-lived compared to the grand totality of things that it almost seems that human history cannot be anything more than a random blip on the long ticker tape of cosmic history. But Moses, while expressing a similar sentiment after being shown a mere fraction of God's creation ("Now, for this cause I know that man is nothing, which thing I never had supposed," Moses 1:10), came to realize that while humans are vanishingly small when compared to the universe, that smallness diverges to infinity once they understand that God created the universe with each one of them in mind. This is another manifestation of God's love and its capacity to make our way to heaven heavenly.

WITH EACH PERSON, PARTICLE, AND WORLD IN MIND

"The idea of primordial revelation," wrote Hugh Nibley, "is that a complete knowledge of the world from its beginning to its end is already written down and has been vouchsafed to certain chosen spirits from time to time, a doctrine familiar to Latter-day Saints."[2] Latter-day scripture portrays Moses, Enoch, Abraham, and the brother of Jared as having received this knowledge in cosmological vision. The experience, of course, was overwhelming, but not for reasons we might suppose. What would it be like to see in one revelatory sweep every person who has lived or will live upon the earth, all the while seeing as well every particle of the earth, as "numberless as the sand upon the sea shore"? (Moses 1:27–28). Mind-dilating, to be sure, but the sheer numerosity of *everything*, when compressed within a single experience, did not of itself elicit expressions of contrition and gratitude. These came with the understanding that all of reality is shot through with the redemptive love of God.

The cosmos is not an arena wherein God's love is put on display, but is itself a manifestation of that love down to the least particle and lowliest sinner. Thus no person and no thing lies beyond the reach of that love, for each is at some level constituted by it.

Enoch grasped the unfathomable nature of God's love when he saw God weeping over a "residue" of sinners who refused to be caught up to Zion (Moses 7:28). But he was puzzled by that love—why would God, the creator of "millions of earths like this," mourn a few backsliders? (v. 30)—until it washed over him in full measure, whereupon he also "wept and stretched forth his arms, and his heart swelled wide as eternity" (v. 41). Although his puzzlement dissipated, he remained enraptured and astonished by the depth of God's love. Similarly, Moses's understanding of the Creation widened without limit when he learned that the entire cosmic project is underwritten by God's love: "For mine own purpose have I made these things. Here is wisdom and it remaineth in me. And by the word of my power, have I created them, which is mine Only Begotten Son, who is full of grace and truth. . . . For behold, this is my work and my glory—to bring to pass the immortality and eternal life of man" (Moses 1:31–32, 39).

So the "grace and truth" of God's love registers in at least three ways: at the level of the individual, at the level of human history where individuals bump and jostle each other across the centuries, and at a cosmic level where worlds pass into and out of existence. The last level is the most surprising perhaps, for though the starry heavens are beautiful, they also seem remote and lifeless. We do not, in any evident way, interact with extraterrestrial beings; our social sphere, wherein we often feel God's love as it is conveyed by others, does not reach that far. Scripture nevertheless indicates that God's love and goodness suffuse all his creation: "And God saw every thing that he had made, and, behold, it was very good" (Genesis 1:31).[3] Perhaps the immense cosmos marks the distance we have yet to travel into "the breadth, and length, and depth, and height" of God's love (Ephesians 3:18).

Which is to suggest that we already live within the cosmic embrace of God's love. In some manner hard to grasp, God fully attends to each person without risking oversight of any other. Here one is reminded of Galileo's comment that "God and Nature are so employed in the governing of human affairs that they could not apply themselves more thereto if they truly had no other care than only that of mankind." To illustrate this thought, Galileo notes the action of light: "And this, I think, I am able to make out by a most pertinent and most noble example, taken from the operation of the Sun's light, which . . . in ripening that bunch of grapes, nay, that single grape, . . . does apply itself so that it could not be more intense, if the sum of all its business had been the maturation of that one grape."[4]

God's love, Galileo is suggesting, is not diminished by distribution or apportionment. It is so superabundant that, like sunlight, it invariably overflows its target—whether one grape or many, whether one person or a vast multitude. The scriptural parallel here is the multiplication miracles when Christ divided a small quantity of food among great crowds of people (see Matthew 14; Mark 8). Afterward his disciples gathered up more food as leftover remnants than was originally given out. Division or sharing led to multiplication, to increase for all, at least within the gospel economy Christ introduced. This is the economy—an infinite sum game—that overwhelms Moses: God's love is so free and gracious that he is able to focus attention on each detail of the world as if it were the whole world.

What the Book of Moses is giving us is a larger window through which to witness the love of God, and through which to contemplate the possibility that God organized the physical universe with no other aim than to save many if not all of his children. Perhaps every detail of one's life, no matter how seemingly trivial or haphazard, serves a salvific purpose, and not just for the individual immediately involved but for all persons, no matter how remote. Perhaps, of course, this is not the case, but the proposition would be consistent with Moses's realization that God is perfectly and simultaneously mindful of large and small. There is no foreground-background duality to his love: all is foreground.

To my knowledge only one person has tried to describe God's creative, salvific work with this possibility in mind, and that was Gottfried Wilhelm Leibniz, the German mathematician and philosopher. I do not believe that Latter-day Saints should uncritically embrace Leibniz, nor should they assume that he was right in all particulars. He was constantly revising his theology and left the project unfinished at death. All the same, his description of God is deeply resonant with Moses's theophany. What is more, Leibniz, in working out his ideas, settles on propositions that readily line up with Latter-day Saint thought. Underpinning these propositions is his belief in a loving God; that is, a God who, while respecting the agency of human beings, would do everything within his power to facilitate their growth and happiness. The divine result would be, as Leibniz first asserted in his 1710 work *Theodicy*, "the best of all possible worlds." Not a perfect world, but a world perfectly suited to our growth and therefore the best possible world given God's aims and his need to respect our free will.

THE BEST POSSIBLE WORLD?

Do we really believe that things will get better in some distant afterlife? Yes, of course, but not in the fairy-tale sense of living happily ever after in a state of unchallenged ease. Rather, we aspire to live "after the manner of happiness" (2 Nephi 5:27) as we confront opposition and evil and, with the help of God, grow into larger spheres of happiness. It seems to me that this latter sensibility is part of the restored gospel, for the Bible tends to characterize happiness as a final destination, a state of arrival wherein we are freed from all care and worry. For example, in the book of Revelation, John sees the New Jerusalem "coming down from God out of heaven" and God dwelling among the persecuted Saints, comforting them. He writes that "God shall wipe away all tears from their eyes; and there shall be no more death, neither sorrow, nor crying, neither shall there be any more pain: for the former things are passed away" (21:2, 4).

I find this beautiful and fully believe that it will happen, just as John foretells. But as a Latter-day Saint I cannot believe that it is the full story. Other scriptural passages suggest that there "must needs be . . . opposition in all things," a principle that Lehi states is essential to our eternal growth (2 Nephi 2:11). What is more, even God appears to struggle with his creation, not just rejoicing in its goodness but also weeping over its sinful inhabitants (see Moses 7:28–37).[5] So while I can appreciate the beauty and power of John's description, and have many times wished away pain in my own life, I can also—owing to Latter-day Saint scripture that slants things differently—acknowledge the cogency of playwright George Bernard Shaw's remark that "a perpetual holiday is a good working definition of hell."[6] Who would want a perfect surcease of pain?

But if pain is something we *do* want, at least in limited quantities, why are we so quick to decry it as part of the imperfection of mortality? Might the truth rather be, as Leibniz proposed, that our present home is the best of all possible worlds when judged by God's world-making, soul-saving criteria? If the universe is a vehicle for making godlike beings, would it help to eliminate, say, bedbugs or the possibility of famine, earthquake, and nuclear holocaust? Or would the elimination of such remove some of the opposition we need to grow through firsthand experience with pain and evil?

It may be that, given our reason for being here, we live in a world *perfectly calculated* to promote our growth. This would be something like Leibniz's world. He assumed that God, possessing the divine wherewithal—the power, knowledge, and benevolent intent—to create the best possible world, would naturally do so. The universe—even in its fallen state, which, after all, is the *via dolorosa* we must travel back to God—would not be a second-rate production; nor would it be marred by haphazard properties that do not dovetail toward God's aim of saving his children.

The task for Leibniz, then, was to determine which criteria God would act on to achieve his purpose. Since antiquity, cosmic harmony—the beauty and order of the physical world—had struck thinkers as the mark of the divine, and Leibniz followed the lead of Plato and generations of subsequent thinkers by proposing that cosmic balance, proportion, and harmony not only reflect God's mind and will but also testify of his existence. He further proposed that harmony arises from the give-and-take of two principles, order and fecundity. Order implies lawfulness, simplicity, and economy, while fecundity connotes variety and richness. Leibniz contended that God achieved maximal cosmic harmony by optimizing the relation between these two principles.

To some degree, order and fecundity work against each other: a world dominated by order would not admit variety of expression, while one utterly characterized by fecundity would be confused and chaotic. So God had to find the perfect balance between these two regulating principles, an immensely complex task, as we shall soon see. Incidentally, this notion of optimizing the relation between order and fecundity has long informed human endeavor. For instance, artists instinctively balance themselves between predictable order and surprising novelty, or between what is sometimes called "white music" (mechanical repetition of tones) and "brown music" (random succession of tones).[7] For Leibniz, the necessary tension between order and fecundity was the recipe for cosmic beauty and goodness, and God implemented that recipe *perfectly* at the world's creation.

The implementation was extremely complex, at least by human standards. It entailed a divine inventory of all possible entities and a review of how those entities would interrelate when placed in differing combinations (i.e., when differently arranged). Each combination represented a possible universe, but in most of these imaginary universes God discovered the incompatibility of two or more entities. The existence of event G, say, ruled out the existence of event Y. Such incompatibilities rendered their respective universes unusable, for given each system's holistic mutuality, the incompatibilities would quickly snowball to involve other entities. And even where there was no incompatibility, there might be other combinations that would allow for greater goodness.

Leibniz goes on to theorize that eventually God hit upon that combination in which all parts or entities were adjusted to each other in the best possible way, and this is the universe he created. Implicit in this process is Leibniz's concept of preestablished harmony. The concept derives from Leibniz's supposition that each possible world is a system of *perfectly* interacting parts. Here is how philosopher Nicholas Rescher explains it: "The substances of each possible world are thus reciprocally adjusted to one another in a thoroughgoing, total way. To use one of Leibniz's favorite metaphors, the substances of a possible world 'mirror' one another in their mutual accommodation."[8] But from this long list of possible worlds, only the best was chosen for actualization.

From a Christian point of view, there appears to be a problem with Leibniz's universe: the apparent lack of freedom. With everything prearranged or preestablished in God's mind, there would seem to be no allowance for spontaneity. Leibniz responded to this objection by explaining that while it is true that every detail of the world was determined at the moment of creation, God's foreknowledge of those details does not necessitate their actualization, just as my knowing the multiplication tables does not necessitate particular arithmetical facts. In either case, outcome is fixed but knowledge thereof is merely incidental.

The analogy is not perfect. In mathematical systems numbers have assigned values, and so the outcomes (answers) they produce when variously combined are reiterative of earlier (though different) arrangements. For example, the number 4 is just another way of saying 2 + 2. And although we may be surprised by a particular mathematical result, it was implicit all along in other terms just waiting, so to speak, to be brought to light by a clever mathematician. This suggests that mathematical systems do not produce novelty, at least not in any absolute sense. Another example: who would ever guess that among twenty-three people there is a better than 50 percent chance that two will share the same birthday? (Indeed, it seems counterintuitive given that the probability of a person being born on any particular day is just 1/365.) Nevertheless, this result is not, in any absolute way, a new fact, even for the person who first arrived at it. It is just a different arrangement or expression of already-known facts—none of which are free to vary.

Within the system God anticipated, however, people are free to grow and vary, and so novelty and spontaneity are real. This difference would have made God's task of discovering the best possible world immeasurably more difficult than any conceivable mathematical calculation. To be sure, the labor may have been so great that nothing but love would have inclined him to undertake it. Like caring parents who attend to every imaginable detail before their children leave home for the first day of kindergarten, God may have similarly anticipated our needs, albeit in a vastly more comprehensive manner. Neither parent (earthly or divine), however, would seek to control everything, though they each would do all within their power to ensure a happy outcome.

Human freedom is the wild card that sets Leibniz's universe apart from mathematical systems. Factoring it in made God's creative work immensely difficult, a true labor of love. Further, it lengthens out the salvific process, for humans are free to proceed at their own pace, and some will progress toward salvation more quickly than others. But God remembers backsliders and has prepared a way for their return, on condition of repentance. To reinvoke Tolstoy's aphorism: "God sees the truth, but waits." He sees or foreknows the end from the beginning owing to the loving care with which he has ordered and harmonized creation; he cannot, however, speed things up, because he will not infringe on our agency. He chooses to wait for us to find our way onto an upward, repentant path so that many if not all of us can ultimately be saved. Again, the rhyme of salvation is long, but it may also be lovingly crafted down to the smallest detail; further, it may be universally harmonized so that each person's quest for happiness redounds in the greatest possible way to the happiness of all people. Leibniz concluded that "if only we could sufficiently understand the order of the universe, we should find that it surpasses all the desires of the wisest [thinkers], and that it is impossible to make it any better than it is, not only for the whole generally, but also for ourselves in particular."[9] Each person is interesting to God because the loss of any individual would render the universe something less than the best of all possible worlds. No person is superfluous; no person represents wasted effort on God's part. The mutual accommodation of every individual thing is so perfectly orchestrated that no person or part can deputize for any other.

WORLDS WITHIN WORLDS, ALL PLEASINGLY DIFFERENT

Leibniz's cosmos incorporates other features that Latter-day Saints generally find praiseworthy. The physical creation is not fully contingent on God, for although God created the universe, he did not create the possibility of its existence. That possibility, along with the numberless other possibilities that God scanned prior to creation, exists independently of God. What is more, God deserves our praise for having selected the best possibility, and even though in this best of all possible worlds evil yet exists, he is not responsible for its existence. Evil, said Leibniz, is built into the creative tension between order and fecundity. God's task, then, was to find that world where evil is minimized while goodness is optimized.

Finally, there is in Leibniz's universe the clear suggestion of unending growth and progress. He took note of the microscopic discoveries of his day, wherein smaller worlds kept showing up as magnifying lenses became more powerful. This for him was evidence of a living, growing cosmos, and some of his statements to this effect resonate with pronouncements offered by Latter-day Saint thinkers. He stated in his *Monadology*, for example:

> From this [the ongoing emplacement or nesting of smaller parts] one sees that there is a whole world of creatures—of organisms, animals, entelechies, and souls—even in the least piece of matter. Every bit of matter can be conceived as a garden full of plants or a pond full of fish. But each branch of the plant, each member of the animal, each drop of its bodily fluids, is also such a garden or such a pond. And though the earth and the air emplaced between the plants of the garden or the water emplaced between the fish of the pond are certainly neither plant nor fish, they contain yet more of them, though mostly of a minuteness imperceptible to us. Thus nothing is fallow, sterile, or dead in the universe; there is no chaos, no disorder save in appearance. It is somewhat like what appears in a distant pond, in which one might see the confused and, so to speak, teeming motion of the pond's fish, without distinguishing the fish themselves.[10]

Worlds within worlds, with no bottommost world because each newly discovered world is a new cosmological narrative embracing other worlds and other narratives as far as the mind can reach. "And there are many kingdoms," we read in the Doctrine and Covenants, "for there is no space in the which there is no kingdom; and there is no kingdom in which there is no space, either a greater or a lesser kingdom" (88:37). Kingdoms or worlds fill up space, but space in turn fills kingdoms, thereby deepening their expanse so that new kingdoms issue up by the courtesy of new space, and so the dialectic of creation continues. By this account, space is not static vastness but creative graciousness, spaciousness, or goodness that is at once spontaneous and inflationary. Hence there are, as Moses tells us, kingdoms or "worlds without number" (Moses 1:33) because the process expresses the pure love of Christ, which issues forth "without compulsory means" (Doctrine and Covenants 121:46).

None of this would make sense if worlds rolled off an assembly line according to a static, repeatable pattern. What would be the purpose of Moses seeing *every* particle and *every* inhabitant of the earth if duplicates existed? According to Leibniz, however, difference, not sameness, is the keynote of creation. Brigham Young expressed the same sentiment:

> Endless variety is stamped upon the works of God's hands. There are no two productions of nature, whether animal, vegetable or mineral, that are exactly alike, and all are crowned with a degree of polish and perfection that cannot be obtained by ignorant man in his most exquisite mechanical productions. Man's machinery makes things alike; God's machinery gives to things which appear alike a pleasing difference.[11]

This may seem an obvious truth, particularly as one leaves the city to witness "endless variety" among the "productions of nature." But even here "man's machinery," which aims at redundancy and sameness, tends to condition our thinking. Every rock reduces to self-similar microconstituents, each atom or subatomic particle being perfectly identical with its namesake counterparts. If you have seen one iron atom you have seen them all, according to science as it has developed in the West since the Greek atomists. Leibniz pushed back against this tradition that reduces visible difference to invisible sameness. Arguing that rational choice is possible only if one option is intrinsically different from another, he insisted that God could not act in a world composed of self-similar building blocks, homogenous units of assembly that science further defined as lifeless. His concern was that with the reduction of difference to sameness, we get not just a world that is boring in its essential details—each part being duplicated again and again ad nauseam—but so boring as to be deadening, even to itself. And with that boredom, we get a world so absent of intrinsic difference as to be a qualitative flatland offering God no traction for making rational choices.

The great upside to this qualitatively redundant world was that it was simple in its construction and therefore in principle fully explicable. As Richard Westfall, an eminent historian of science, put it, the older vision of reality was one in which every physical body possessed "active principle, which partook at least to some extent of the characteristics of mind or spirit"; the view of modern science, however, "excise[d] every trace of the psychic from material nature with surgical precision, leaving it a lifeless field knowing only the brute blows of inert chunks of matter. It was a conception of nature startling in its bleakness—but admirably contrived for the [explanatory] purposes of modern science."[12]

As depressing as it may sound, this is the worldview that we have inherited from classical physics and that has seeped into virtually every other field of science so as to desacralize and render monotonous our vision of nature. Because it pays no allegiance to a loving Creator, we often find ourselves switching tracks as we contemplate nature from first a religious and then a scientific perspective. Leibniz, however, believed that intellect could be folded into faith to empower both endeavors, and not just after the two had staked out opposing truth claims.

Like other scientists of his era, Leibniz was trying to rethink the thoughts of God at the creation of the universe. But his great philosophical antagonist, Isaac Newton, was trying to do the same thing, and he came up with a worldview that gave priority to sameness rather than difference. So much for reading God's mind, and so much for the pretense that scientists read the text of nature without philosophical interpolation. Neither Newton nor Leibniz could fully resist the early modern infatuation with machines and the follow-on notion of a clockwork universe operating with perfect regularity according to well-understood mechanical principles. This outlook morphed into the deism of eighteenth-century thought—the view that God had wound up the universe like a clock and then let it operate without outside (divine) interference—but Leibniz's own vision, which saw mechanism as an expression of deeper principles, was much more richly nuanced. For our purposes, his signal contribution was the argument that diversity is the primordial intrigue of reality. Without the spontaneous efflorescence of difference, novelty, and surprise, everything *really* would be lifeless and no philosopher or scientist would exist to lament or take delight in that fact.

CREATIVE DIFFERENCE

While I have no way of knowing whether Leibniz's outlook is correct, I like to keep it in mind because it purports that no detail of reality is irrelevant or inadvertent. Every detail brims with divine love, so much so that even small, seemingly insignificant things turn out to be inexhaustibly deep reservoirs of creative possibility. Perhaps if we could reverse the nesting process we would see God's love exploding out of every pore and particle of reality, no matter how minute. In any event, Latter-day Saint thinkers have proposed that there is more going on with so-called brute matter than meets the eye. Brigham Young, for example, stated that "there is not a particle of element which is not filled with life. . . . There is life in all matter, throughout the vast extent of all the eternities; it is in the rock, the sand, the dust, . . . [the] air."[13] And Elder Neal A. Maxwell insisted that life becomes real as it surrenders itself to God, which surrender entails the flowering of individual difference. "Some presume," he said "that we will lose our individuality if we are totally swallowed up [by God's will], when actually our individuality is enhanced by submissiveness and by righteousness and by being swallowed up in the will of the Father. It's sin that grinds us down to a single plane, down to sameness and to monotony."[14]

In the Doctrine and Covenants we read of a white stone "given to each of those who come into the celestial kingdom, whereon is a new name written, which no man knoweth save he that receiveth it" (130:10–11). The white stone is also mentioned in the book of Revelation, along with a similar promise to those who are faithful (2:17). What would be the point of receiving such in confidence with God if every new name were the same? C. S. Lewis developed this idea:

> What can be more a man's own than this new name which even in eternity remains a secret between God and him? And what shall we take this secrecy to mean? Surely, that each of the redeemed shall forever know and praise some one aspect of the divine beauty better than any other creature can. Why else were individuals created, but that God loving all infinitely, should love each differently?[15]

Lewis maintains that we best glorify God when we symphonically and synergistically blend our differences. This is the way of the gospel, and also the way of nature. To be sure, there are unvarying standards that structure the world, constants and regularities that give nature its predictability. But there are also moments of escape and surprise that track back to difference. Since the late nineteenth century many of the so-called laws of nature, once viewed as absolutely binding and determinative of given results, have been reconceptualized as matters of statistical likelihood. There is no nature-ordained mandate that an ice cube will melt when dropped into a glass of water, but the probability of its not melting is unimaginably more remote than shuffling playing cards and getting a perfectly ordered deck. Put differently, laws of nature are now often regarded as descriptions of what will probably happen, not prescriptions of what must happen; and surprise, some have suggested, fills the space between prescription and description. To follow scientific philosopher Charles Sanders Peirce, this is where nature goes "sporting" to produce "infinitesimal departures from law continually, and great ones [like ourselves] with infinite frequency."[16] Such departures are the stuff of pleasing difference, which is integral to God's work, according to Brigham Young, and the reason God's eye lights upon every person, part, and particle of creation—because each is pleasingly different. Each finds a place in the universe, and in the heart of God, no other can find.

Snowflakes illustrate this principle. Although trillions fall every year, no two are exactly alike. Each begins as a simple six-sided crystal that then falls along a unique path whose microconditions shape and develop the flake differently. The world is such that the likelihood of two flakes falling along identical paths even for a single millimeter is vanishingly small. And yet all snowflakes share a common architecture whose infinitely variegated beauty bespeaks a larger theme. "They are about a tenth of an inch in diameter," wrote Henry David Thoreau, "perfect little wheels with six spokes . . . whirling to earth, pronouncing thus, with emphasis, the number six. Order, *kóσmos*. . . . And they all sing, melting as they sing of the mysteries of the number six—six, six, six."[17] There is a law behind all this, Thoreau insists, but it is not geared toward mechanical, mind-numbing production of sameness. Rather, it excites the mind heavenward by allowing space for creative difference in its repetitive elaboration of hexagonal crystals: "How full of the creative genius is the air in which these are generated! I should hardly admire more, if real stars fell and lodged on my coat. Nature is full of genius, full of divinity, so that not a snow-flake escapes its fashioning hand."[18] As Leibniz proposed, God's creation strikes the perfect balance between order and fecundity; thus the world is "full of genius, full of divinity," so that nothing, ourselves included, "escapes its fashioning hand."

NOTES

1. Leo Tolstoy, "God Sees the Truth, but Waits," *Walk in the Light and Twenty-Three Tales*, trans. Louise and Aylmer Maude (Maryknoll, NY: Orbis, 2003), 69–77.
2. Hugh W. Nibley, "Genesis of the Written Word," *Nibley on the Timely and the Timeless: Classic Essays of Hugh W. Nibley* (Provo, UT: Religious Studies Center, Brigham Young University, 1978), 110.
3. Note also that in the original Greek the word for "world" in John 3:16 ("For God so loved the world, that he gave his only begotten Son . . .") is *kosmos*, which is cognate with the English *cosmos*. One may accordingly think of the universe—the whole of God's creation—as the object of God's redeeming love.
4. Galileo Galilei, *Dialogue on the Great World Systems*, ed. Giorgio de Santillana (Chicago: University of Chicago Press, 1953), 378–79.
5. See Terryl Givens and Fiona Givens, *The God Who Weeps: How Mormonism Makes Sense of Life* (Salt Lake City: Ensign Peak, 2012).
6. George Bernard Shaw, *Misalliance*, in *Misalliance, The Dark Lady of the Sonnets, and Fanny's First Play, with a Treatise on Parents and Children* (Cambridge: Wildside, 1914), xlv.
7. Martin Gardner, "Mathematical Games: White and Brown Music, Fractal Curves and One-Over-F Fluctuations," *Scientific American* 238, no. 4 (April 1978): 16–32.
8. Nicholas Rescher, *Leibniz: An Introduction to His Philosophy* (Oxford, UK: Basil Blackwell, 1979), 17.
9. Quoted in Nicholas Rescher, *G. W. Leibniz's Monadology: An Edition for Students* (Pittsburgh, PA: University of Pittsburgh Press, 1991), 295.
10. Quoted in Rescher, *G. W. Leibniz's Monadology*, 26.
11. Brigham Young, in *Journal of Discourses*, 26 vols. (London: Latter-day Saints' Book Depot, 1854–86), 9:369–70.
12. Richard S. Westfall, *The Construction of Modern Science: Mechanisms and Mechanics* (New York: John Wiley and Sons, 1971), 31.
13. Brigham Young, in *Journal of Discourses*, 3:277.
14. Elder Maxwell's remarks were delivered at the FARMS Annual Recognition Banquet, September 27, 1991, Brigham Young University campus; quoted in Daniel C. Peterson, "Elder Neal A. Maxwell

on Consecration, Scholarship, and the Defense of the Kingdom," *Interpreter: A Journal of Mormon Scripture* 7 (2013): xvii.
15. C. S. Lewis, *The Problem of Pain* (New York: Touchstone, 1996), 134.
16. Charles Sanders Peirce, "The Architecture of Theories" and "The Doctrine of Necessity Examined," in *Philosophers of Process*, ed. Douglas Browning and William T. Myers (New York: Fordham University Press, 1998), 8 and 26 respectively.
17. Henry David Thoreau, *The Heart of Thoreau's Journals*, ed. Odell Shepherd (New York: Dover Publications, 1961), 149–50.
18. Thoreau, *The Heart of Thoreau's Journals*, 149.

CHAPTER 3

Losing Self, Finding Peace

If we thought of life as a gift, we might not demand nearly as much from it. And if we lived more graciously, giving of ourselves more freely to the well-being of others, many of our personal concerns would disappear, and life would become easier for all.

—Lowell C. Bennion

The Apostle Paul taught that though we are all different, there is no room in the gospel for self-elevation. He reminds fellow Christians that while their bodies are composed of different parts, none are fully independent of the others. "So we, being many," he continues, "are one body in Christ, and every one members one of another" (see Romans 12:4–5; 1 Corinthians 12). The awkward *members* indicates that each person leans into all the others, and they into her, just as every body part leans into all the others to seamlessly constitute a living body. Individuals exist, but in interactive unity, not as self-contained beings whose inimitability gives them reason to show off or say to others, "I have no need of you" (1 Corinthians 12:21).

In this regard, Paul speaks of the gifts of the Spirit, which are variously given to individuals for the building up of the Church and the mutual edification of all its members. According to *The Abingdon Bible Commentary*, "the health of the whole body depends upon the faithfulness with which each [member] makes use of his special endowment."[1] Thus, one's talents are not to be trumpeted as individual achievements; they are to be seen as God-given and consequently directed toward his ends. In brief, individual differences are pitched toward the salvation of the entire body.

Remembering our obligation to others in the face of our uniqueness is not always easy. Sometimes we want to dance in the end zone. But the antidote to excessive self-celebration is happiness and humility, which C. S. Lewis describes as a single package. In his book *Mere Christianity*, he ventures that a humble person is a happy, self-forgetful person—a person unmindful of his or her own humility.

> Do not imagine that if you meet a really humble man he will be what most people call "humble" nowadays: he will not be a sort of greasy, smarmy person, who is always telling you that, of course, he is nobody. Probably all you will think about him is that he seemed a cheerful, intelligent chap who took a real interest in what *you* said to *him*. If you do dislike him it will be because you feel a little envious of anyone who seems to enjoy life so easily. He will not be thinking about humility: he will not be thinking about himself at all.[2]

Herein lies a deep Christian truth: those who achieve this blessed state of not thinking of themselves are blessed or happy in that very moment. This is not to say that future blessings will not also be theirs, only that in the present moment they are caught up to a happiness undiluted by concern for self.

The beatitudes of the Sermon on the Mount announce this principle. They describe various gospel virtues—meekness, mercy, forbearance, and so on—as having intrinsic power to immediately happify those who practice them. These virtues were part of the "scandal" of the gospel,[3] as the Apostle Paul put it, because they called into question cultural norms that associated happiness with worldly might, wealth, and advancement of self. Such norms were "the wisdom of this world" (who, after all, would think that happiness could be found amid want, persecution, and grief?), while the beatitudes were part of "the foolishness of God" (1 Corinthians 3:19; 1:25).

The word *Blessed* that begins each beatitude indicates a present condition, scholars tell us. It marks the beatific joy that accompanies Christian discipleship while recognizing that such joy, though complete at the moment, continues to grow over time like the seed of faith that Alma the Younger described. Thus each beatitude links a present state of happiness to the future realization of yet greater happiness, the former moment blossoming into the latter. One beatitude, for instance, states that those who are pure in heart shall see God, but the *Blessed* that begins the beatitude denotes happiness or blessedness right from the start *and* the natural expansion of that happiness as the purifying process unfolds toward the sublime moment of beholding the face of God. Alma correspondingly noted that even a tiny seed of faith—nothing more than a "particle of faith" (Alma 32:27)—was not something to be endured or suffered. Rather, once acted upon, it brings joy: "it beginneth to enlarge my soul, yea, it beginneth to enlighten my understanding, yea, it beginneth to be delicious to me" (v. 28).

Sometimes, of course, we must endure trials of faith, but the simple act of exercising faith in God—independent of whatever trial we may be passing through—is not onerous. Because it is an intrinsically good endeavor, it imparts strength and lifts one's spirit. This is to propose that God never leaves us comfortless; there is comfort and blessing to be found in living his commandments, and such kicks in the moment we decide to keep those commandments. "Because personal revelation is a constantly renewable source of strength, it is possible to feel bathed in help even during turbulent times," stated Relief Society General President Julie B. Beck.[4] Or, as the medieval Catholic thinker Catherine of Siena insisted, "All the way to heaven is heaven." Once we step on the gospel path, the ground beneath our feet has a different, more vibrant bounce. This bounce is sometimes called grace, and it is the very taproot of our salvation. Without it we could never step on the gospel path in the first place.

THE GRACE-FILLED DELICIOUSNESS OF THE GOSPEL

The scriptures make this point about heaven-sent strength abundantly clear. When Paul instructs the Saints at Philippi to "work out [their] own salvation with fear and trembling," he may seem to be casting the entire burden of salvation on weak, erring human beings and leaving them bereft of heavenly help. But this is not the whole story, for he immediately adds, "For it is God which worketh in you both to will and to do of his good pleasure" (Philippians 2:12–13).

LOSING SELF, FINDING PEACE

Now there is reason to believe that God will make up the difference between our weakness and his strength.

Or *help us* make up the difference. It is often hard to know in the working out of our salvation where we end and God begins. We are, Nephi said, saved by grace "after all we can do" (2 Nephi 25:23); but as Moroni also taught, we are saved by grace amid the things we *cannot* do. To his distress, Moroni felt he could not leave a powerful written testimony of Jesus Christ. It was then that the Lord told him that it didn't matter; what mattered was the humility Moroni felt upon realizing his weakness, for that humility made him receptive to the Lord's saving grace, and in that moment his weak testimony was made strong (see Ether 12:23–28). In my mind there is no testimony more beautiful and moving in all of scripture than that given by Moroni at the end of chapter 12 of the book of Ether. After declaring that he will meet us at "the judgment-seat of Christ" (v. 38), he states:

> And then shall ye know that I have seen Jesus, and that he hath talked with me face to face, and that he told me in plain humility, even as a man telleth another in mine own language, concerning these things; and only a few have I written, because of my weakness in writing. And now, I would commend you to seek this Jesus of whom the prophets and apostles have written, that the grace of God the Father, and also the Lord Jesus Christ, and the Holy Ghost, which beareth record of them, may be and abide in you forever. Amen. (vv. 39–41)

Just before expressing this testimony, Moroni states that he was "comforted" when he learned that God would turn his weakness into strength, but the comfort he feels is not connected with concern for his own salvation (Ether 12:29). Rather, his concern all along has been for those who will come later—that is, the descendants of those who will survive the Lamanite slaughter and, in the far-off future, the Gentiles among whom the Book of Mormon will make its latter-day appearance. Moroni, as noted earlier, is stretched out along the long arc of God's love. If he is anxious, he is anxious for others. If he cannot fall asleep at night, it is not because he is reliving some private narrative of the day's events, but because he, like Nephi, is pleading with the Lord on behalf of thousands, if not millions, of others. In his farewell words, Nephi states, "I pray continually for them [future generations of Nephites, Lamanites, and Gentiles] by day, and mine eyes water my pillow by night, because of them; and I cry unto my God in faith, and I know that he will hear my cry" (2 Nephi 33:3).

This sounds heavy. Who could bear up for very long under the strain of so much concern? Probably no normal man or woman. Note, however, that at least in their later years Nephi and Moroni do not seem to be weighed down with concern for their own salvation. Nothing they record indicates they are anxious about their own eternal welfare. Perhaps having surmounted that concern, they have been delivered by God's love into a wider sphere of action. One thinks here of Joseph Smith's words: "A man filled with the love of God, is not content with blessing his family alone, but ranges through the whole world anxious to bless the whole human race."[5] Not that Nephi, Moroni, or Joseph Smith traveled the world over, but their focus was "the whole human race," whether dead, living, or yet unborn.

Here again C. S. Lewis's point about the happy, humble, self-forgetful person registers. At what point in our gospel progression do we begin to give up our anxious, self-centered quest for salvation? Evidently when the grace-filled deliciousness of the gospel has so expanded our souls that we want to share it with others. After making his way to the tree of life and tasting of the fruit that represented the love of God, Lehi did not continue feasting alone. His solitary quest suddenly expanded to include family: "As I partook of the fruit thereof it filled my soul with exceedingly great joy; wherefore I began to be desirous that my family should partake of it also" (1 Nephi 8:12). At first his concern rested only on members of his immediate family, but it globalized in time to embrace generations unborn, as evidenced by the final blessings he pronounced on his grandchildren and their posterity. These blessings implicitly acknowledged the waywardness of his two older sons, neither of whom had partaken of the fruit of the tree of life in Lehi's vision, and included a promise of deliverance to their descendants from the curse of unbelief that Laman and Lemuel had inaugurated: "Wherefore, if ye are cursed, behold, I leave my blessing upon you, that the cursing may be taken from you and be answered upon the heads of your parents" (2 Nephi 4:6).

Lehi's expansive concern paralleled that of the once-reprobate sons of Mosiah who had been snatched by the love of God into light and joy. They "could not bear that any human soul should perish," should suffer the calamity of not being transported by divine love just as they had been (Mosiah 28:3). Accordingly, they devoted the remainder of their lives to missionary work, hoping to pass on the miracle of God's saving love to others and, it seems, no longer concerned about their own salvation.

FINDING HAPPINESS

Paramount concern with *my* salvation is a good place to start, but the straight and narrow gospel path engenders wide concern for others. We cannot stay on that path for very long without experiencing brief but liberating moments of ego oblivion. Jesus stated, "Whosoever shall seek to save his life shall lose it; and whosoever shall lose his life shall preserve it" (Luke 17:33). Unending concern for *my* salvation puts one at risk of narcissistic self-destruction. Letting larger concerns override my inclination to look in the mirror, though, works to my salvific advantage, but only because I take no interest in self-advancement. When asked whether self-aggrandizement was a true principle, Joseph Smith stated that it was, but then added that it "may be indulged upon only one rule or plan—and that is to elevate, benefit, and bless others first. If you will elevate others, the very work itself will exalt you. Upon no other plan can a man justly and permanently aggrandize himself."[6]

Surely this is something we all know at some level. "The greatest fulfillment in life comes by rendering service to others, and not by being obsessed with 'what's in it for me,'" taught President James E. Faust while serving in the Church's First Presidency.[7] Indeed, Satan is our best example of how spiritual destruction overtakes those excessively concerned with individual exaltation. The quest for preeminence, especially spiritual preeminence, is sure to backfire, if only because that quest lives from the aspiration to rise above others. Satan was like the man who preemptively sat in the highest seat at the wedding feast, only to be removed from his place by the master of the feast (see Luke 14:7–11). Of course, few of us would openly angle for such a seat, but perhaps in small ways we do seek to elevate ourselves above others. This, however, can never work to our lasting advantage because the calculation to advance oneself at the expense of others reenacts in miniature Satan's grand aspiration.

If salvation founders on the reef of self-calculation, so also does happiness. The deliberate, all-consuming aspiration to be happy is, in fact, a recipe for unhappiness. "Happiness is not a goal, it is a by-product," observed former First Lady Eleanor Roosevelt. "Paradoxically, the one sure way not to be happy is deliberately to map out a way of life in which one would please oneself completely and exclusively."[8] Leo Tolstoy expressed it this way: "Happiness founded upon vanity [self-interest] is destroyable by the same."[9] And this from the Latter-day Saint scholar and poet Arthur Henry King: "If we aim at self-fulfillment, we shall never be fulfilled. If we aim at education, we shall never become educated. If we aim at salvation, we shall never be saved. These things are indirect, supreme results of doing something else; and the something else is service, it is righteousness, it is trying to do the right thing, the thing that needs to be done at each moment."[10]

These expressions coincide with the scriptural suggestion that happiness arrives in the wake of selfless behavior, although how quickly it arrives is not ours to say. Thus we live "after the manner of happiness" (2 Nephi 5:27), implicitly recognizing that our righteous actions conduce to happiness without constraining it. Happiness, like all things spiritual, springs up "without compulsory means" (Doctrine and Covenants 121:46). We can no more command it than we can command the wind, which Jesus likened to the saving spirit or the breath of life when he explained the principle of baptism to Nicodemus: "The wind [*pneuma* in Greek] bloweth where its listeth, and thou hearest the sound thereof, but canst not tell whence it cometh, and whither it goeth; so is everyone that is born of the Spirit [*pneuma*]" (John 3:8). Thus there is always a spontaneous, gift-like quality to spiritual happiness answering to the fact that it is, after all, a gift from heaven. Accordingly, there is some aspect to it that overflows our expectations and is happily unpredictable and noncompulsory in its manner of arrival. Though we cannot fully control how and when such happy accidents will befall us, we do know that living the gospel makes us more accident-prone. "Most of all," stated Elder Neal A. Maxwell, "revelation requires us to have a sufficient degree of personal righteousness, so that on occasion revelation may come to the righteous, unsolicited."[11]

My point is that, unlike most other things we aspire to accomplish, happiness and salvation cannot be taken by frontal assault. To use Roosevelt's word, they are *by-products* of selfless behavior, gifts that come to us "without compulsory means" as we transcend our selfish need for them. Jesus Christ is our great exemplar here. In his epistle to the Philippians, Paul wrote that Christ, though in "the form of God," "made himself of no reputation, and took upon him the form of a servant, and was made in the likeness of men: and being found in fashion as a man, he humbled himself, and became obedient unto death, even the death of the cross" (2:5–8). Though salvation was his for the asking, he did not ask for it, but rather meekly submitted himself to the anguish and ignominy of Gethsemane and Golgotha.

This is the nature of Christlike love: as Paul said, it "seeketh not her own" (1 Corinthians 13:5). Because it is self-forgetful, it releases us from the cares besetting those who struggle for happiness according to the "wisdom of the world"—that is, via the acquisition of personal wealth, influence, and status. More than that, it delivers us over to the "foolishness of God" whereby we taste divine life in the here and now. "Take my yoke upon you, and learn of me," said Jesus, "for I am meek and lowly in heart: and ye shall find rest unto your souls." And then these amazing words: "For my yoke is easy, and my burden is light" (Matthew 11:29–30).

"MY BURDEN IS LIGHT"

With so much at stake and so many wayward people to worry about and pray for, how could Christ's disciples find his yoke easy and his burden light? Perhaps in the same way Moroni found comfort in realizing that divine grace had made up the difference between his own weakness and God's power to save. That power came to his rescue as he was trying to rescue others (in the distant future). When Moroni lamented that his own strength and skill were not up to the task of conveying a powerful witness of God's goodness, the Lord comforted him by promising to make up the shortfall. This is the manifestation of grace that so moves and touches Moroni—the divine assurance that his weakness will not be charged to his account at the last day. Indeed, it will somehow, in God's economy, be credited to Moroni as righteousness and strength.

God, acting from limitless strength born of sacrificial love, is kind, forgiving, and strengthening to those who acknowledge their weakness. Satan, by contrast, accused his brethren "day and night" (Revelation 12:10), wishing to tear them down and having no strength to share with others because he had tried the ill-fated shortcut of exalting himself before working to exalt others. But no accusations await the humble followers of Christ. They have tapped into the "pure river of water of life" mentioned by John in the book of Revelation: "clear as crystal, proceeding out of the throne of God and of the Lamb" (Revelation 22:1). They know the peace that Jesus left in this world—not the hit-and-miss peace that "the world giveth," but the lasting peace that floods one's soul upon realizing that in the big picture of things Christ has taken care of everything we could possibly worry about. "Let not your heart be troubled, neither let it be afraid," Christ told his disciples on the eve of his departure (John 14:27). "These things I have spoken unto you, that in me ye might have peace. In the world ye shall have tribulation: but be of good cheer; I have overcome the world" (16:33).

To be sure, the peace of which Jesus speaks is hard to hold on to amid the turmoil of life, but that is because our faith wavers. When the waves of the storm-tossed sea begin to frighten us, we sink like Peter back into the cares of the world, into a milieu of doubt, fear, and uncertainty. The gospel, however, impels us toward a higher, truer understanding of things. "We speak the wisdom of God," wrote Paul, ". . . even the hidden wisdom, which God ordained before the world unto our glory: which none of the princes of this world knew." This wisdom, Paul continues, could never be surmised from existing social and political structures, for such instantiate the uncertainties that the gospel dissipates. That wisdom comes only as God reveals it "unto us by his Spirit: for the Spirit searcheth all things, yea, the deep things of God" (1 Corinthians 2:7–8, 10).

The peace of God signifies freedom from care, a leave-taking of the anxious concerns, physical and spiritual, that characterize normal experience. Jesus condemned the scribes and Pharisees for adding to these concerns by laying heavy religious burdens on others, "grievous to be borne," while making no effort to ease the burdens of everyday life (Matthew 23:4). Jesus, on the other hand, advocated the lifting of burdens and, quite extraordinarily, a care-free life ("Take no thought for your life, what ye shall eat, or what ye shall drink," 6:25) patterned after the fowls of the air and the lilies of the field, which subsisted from moment to moment on God's overflowing goodness. This, of course, is not the whole story, for we are also commanded to labor, to prepare for times of need, and to work to overcome our sinful tendencies. But it is, I believe, the higher part of the story; that is, the rest of God to be found in this world, which rest overtakes us as we lay down the burden of our own salvation while, like Jesus, lifting others' burdens. Thus the gospel path is both hard and easy; hard because it entails assuming others' burdens, but easy because by those burdens we win fellowship with the Lord Jesus Christ, who, unlike the scribes and Pharisees, takes away burdens and gives rest.

"Be careful for nothing," wrote Paul, "but in every thing by prayer and supplication with thanksgiving let your requests be made known unto God" (Philippians 4:6). The translation is a bit stilted here, for in telling the Saints at Philippi to "be careful for nothing," Paul was not advocating inattentiveness to everyday needs. Rather, he was counseling the Saints to lighten their cares by prayerfully sharing them with the Lord. He didn't promise that those cares would go away, but he did insist that the blessing of such sharing is incalculably great: "And the peace of God, which passeth all understanding, shall keep your hearts and minds through Christ Jesus" (v. 7).

We could never experience this peace in an abstract or theoretical way, but only as our mortal hurts compel us to cry out to God, who, as the philosopher Alfred North Whitehead said, "is the great companion—the fellow sufferer who understands."[12] And, I might add, who gives relief that "passeth all understanding." If we invite God into our lives, our earthly hurts can function as kindling that catches fire as he draws near. Thereby we realize that God is not distant after all, though the erstwhile sense of his remoteness is the backdrop against which our realization of God's nearness flares into existence. Thus, as Lehi stated, there is "opposition in all things" and existence is "a compound in one" (2 Nephi 2:11). Our separation from God is the precondition for our rescue by him, which rescue is deeply felt, and deeply treasured, in the midst of mortal extremity. Indeed, by that rescue we are lifted up to the sublimity of Paul's witness of Christ in his epistle to the Philippians: "For to me to live is Christ, and to die is gain" (1:21). In Christ we live, die, and live anew.

NOTES

1. *The Abingdon Bible Commentary*, ed. Frederick Carl Eiselen, Edwin Lewis, and David G. Downey (Garden City, NY: Doubleday, 1957), 1187.
2. C. S. Lewis, *Mere Christianity* (New York: Collier Books, 1960), 114.
3. The word *scandal* derives from the Greek word *skandalon*, meaning an "offense" or "stumbling block" and translated as *stumblingblock* in 1 Corinthians 1:23 (King James Version).
4. Julie B. Beck, "And upon the Handmaids in Those Days Will I Pour Out My Spirit," *Ensign*, May 2010.
5. Joseph Smith, History, 1838–1856, volume C-1 [2 November 1838–31 July 1842], 1115, *The Joseph Smith Papers*, https://www.josephsmithpapers.org/. Joseph Smith continues: "[T]his has been your feeling and caused you to forego the pleasures of home, that you might be a blessing to others, who are candidates for immortality, but strangers to truth." Brigham Young stated: "Every person that confines his thoughts and labors to happifying his own family and

immediate friends will come far short of performing the duties devolving upon him. Every sentiment and feeling should be to cleanse the earth from wickedness, to purify the people, sanctify the nations, gather the nations of Israel home, redeem and build up Zion, redeem Jerusalem and gather the Jews there, and establish the reign and kingdom of God on earth." In *Journal of Discourses*, 8:294.
6. Quoted in Hyrum L. Andrus and Helen Mae Andrus, *They Knew the Prophet* (Salt Lake City: Bookcraft, 1974), 61.
7. James E. Faust, "What's in It for Me?," *Ensign*, November, 2002, 22.
8. Eleanor Roosevelt, *You Learn by Living* (Louisville, KY: Westminster John Knox Press, 1960), 95.
9. *The Diaries of Leo Tolstoy: Youth, 1847–1852*, trans. C. J. Hogarth and A. Sirnis (London: J. M. Dent and Sons, 1917), 98.
10. Arthur Henry King, *The Abundance of the Heart* (Salt Lake City: Bookcraft, 1986), 255.
11. Neal A. Maxwell, "Revelation," *First Worldwide Leadership Training Meeting, January 11, 2003* (Salt Lake City: The Church of Jesus Christ of Latter-day Saints, 2003), 5, accessible at https://laconicisms.files.wordpress.com/2013/12/first-worldwide-leadership-training-meeting-11-jan-2003.pdf.
12. Alfred North Whitehead, *Process and Reality*, ed. David Ray Griffin and Donald W. Sherburne (New York: Free Press, 1978), 351.

CHAPTER 4

The Witness and Promise of Nature

The smell of the earth is good. It is apparent that there is no death.
—Edna St. Vincent Millay, "Spring"

Who, in looking upon the earth as it ascends in the scale of the universe, does not desire to keep pace with it, that when it shall be classed in its turn, among the dazzling orbs of the blue vault of heaven, shining forth in all the splendours of celestial glory, he may find himself proportionably advanced . . . ?
—Orson Pratt, in *Journal of Discourses*, 1:333

We are thus for ever in presence of miracles; and as old Nathan said, the greatest of all miracles is that the genuine miracles should be so familiar.
—Samuel Alexander, "Natural Piety"

In the book of John we read, "Then said Jesus to those Jews which believed on him, If ye continue in my word, then are ye my disciples indeed; and ye shall know the truth, and the truth shall make you free" (8:31–32). The oft-remarked paradox here is that obedience or bondage to the word of God becomes our passport to freedom. When seen aright, mortality is at once tight confinement and liberating chrysalis, and "those things by which the world is bound, by those very things may its bondage be released."[1] This release, however, presupposes death and rebirth—the dying of the natural man and the gathering up from the ashes thereof a new creature in Christ. Jesus compared the process to a seed buried in the ground: "Except a corn of wheat fall into the ground and die, it abideth alone: but if it die, it bringeth forth much fruit" (John 12:24).

The death of a single kernel of wheat resets the miracle of creation. From a single seed of wheat comes a stalk of wheat—much fruit—and then the miracle may repeat itself again and again in an ever-expanding way. After growing a tomato plant from a single seed and realizing that the plant produced many seeds, each embryonically a plant with the same seed-producing potential, a seven-year-old granddaughter of President M. Russell Ballard observed, "And if all of those seeds were planted and grew more tomatoes, and you planted all of those seeds, in a few seasons you would have millions of tomatoes."[2] But of course, as Jesus stated, each seed must die, or give itself over to something bigger than itself, for the seed that refuses to die fruitlessly hangs on to itself and thereby abides alone.

The saving grace of mortality is that it is passage into something infinitely greater. The death-bound mortal body, said Paul, is "sown in weakness" but "raised in power" (1 Corinthians 15:43). While Brigham Young stated that our dead bodies are planted like seeds in the earth to come forth in the Resurrection,[3] he also taught that the earth experience is the backdrop for the exhilaration that overtakes our spirits when they are released from their bodily confinement.

THE WITNESS AND PROMISE OF NATURE

Speaking at the funeral of Thomas Williams, President Young insisted that when we have crossed into the next world "we shall turn round and look upon it [mortality] and think, . . . why this is the greatest advantage of my whole existence, for I have passed from a state of sorrow, grief, mourning, woe, misery, pain, anguish and disappointment into a state of existence, where I can enjoy life to the fullest extent as far as that can be done without a body." And feeling liberated from our sluggish, pain-ridden bodies, we will feel to rejoice, "My spirit is set free, I thirst no more, I want to sleep no more, I hunger no more, I tire no more, I run, I walk, I labor, I go, I come, I do this, I do that, whatever is required of me, nothing like pain or weariness, I am full of life, full of vigor, and I enjoy the presence of my heavenly Father, by the power of his Spirit."[4]

All the same, in time we will cease rejoicing in the freedom of the spirit and will consider "the long absence of [our] spirits from [our] bodies to be a bondage" while yearning for the "day of redemption"—that is, restoration and resurrection (Doctrine and Covenants 45:17; 138:50). So long as physical element and spirit remain apart, "man cannot receive a fulness of joy" (93:34). Until that indissoluble restoration occurs, therefore, we find ourselves handicapped either by the infirmities of the body or by no body at all as the spirit flies free of mortal hardship, albeit *unredeemed* mortal hardship. What we await is the glorious moment when the dross of our earthly experience will be changed to gold and, in "the twinkling of an eye" according to Paul, we "shall be raised incorruptible, and we shall be changed" (1 Corinthians 15:52).

But before the Resurrection our earthly experience, Paul also said, may be eased and enriched by the Holy Ghost, whose witness is an earnest or promissory note—and a foretaste—of our future life with God, if we are faithful. The thrill of the Spirit testifies that God has "put his Spirit in our hearts as a deposit, guaranteeing what is to come" (2 Corinthians 1:22, New International Version).[5]

Said another way, the restored gospel of Jesus Christ enwraps us in truth—not, however, to confine us, but to ease and brighten our mortal circumstance by affording us moments of celestial refreshment along the way. Hence, all the way to heaven is heaven. If mortality is a kind of prison house, the gospel helps us find the chinks and breathing holes therein. In the process we are liberated by the very things that bind us, by our intimacy with hurt and frailty, and thereby we come to know the two-way miracle of God's saving love. "All beings, to be crowned with crowns of glory and eternal lives," taught Brigham Young, "must in their infantile weakness begin, with regard to their trials, the day of their probation: they must descend below all things, in order to ascend above all things."[6]

This is God's saving love because he was the first to open the path. Thirty-three years before the resurrected Christ ascended into heaven to stand at the right hand of his Father, he was born in a lowly stable. And while Luke reports that as Jesus grew he "increased in wisdom and stature, and in favour with God and man" (Luke 2:52), Isaiah describes the paradoxical, pain-filled complexity of his life. "Who hath believed our report?" asks Isaiah, as though it is too wondrous to be believed that someone so lowly, so accursed, and so cast off from the power structures of human society would take up the burden of salvation of those who rejected him. Jesus, the Messiah, will "grow up . . . as a tender plant, and as a root out of a dry ground: he hath no form nor comeliness; and when we shall see him, there is no beauty that we should desire him." Further, he will know firsthand the heartache of loneliness, grief, and steadfast social disfavor: "He is despised and rejected of men; a man of sorrows, and acquainted with grief: and we hid as it were our faces from him; he was despised, and we esteemed him not." Finally, in some way hard to comprehend, he will be the sacrificial lamb foreordained to bear our griefs and carry our sorrows and to be "wounded for our transgressions" and "bruised for our iniquities," though we have "esteem[ed] him stricken, smitten of God, and afflicted." In brief, "with his stripes [wounds] we are healed" (Isaiah 53:1–5).

None of this makes sense if we subtract ourselves from the picture Isaiah paints; that is, if we assume that, not having lived at the time of Christ, we play no role in his humiliation and sorrow. Elsewhere Christ lets us know that his descent below all things is the nature and condition of everyday life: "Inasmuch as ye have done it unto one of the least of these my brethren, ye have done it unto me" (Matthew 25:40), whether we have chosen to help and uplift others or, as Moroni put it, opted to "adorn" ourselves "with that which hath no life, and . . . suffer[ed] the hungry, and the needy, and the naked, and the sick and the afflicted to pass by . . . and notice[ed] them not" (Mormon 8:39).

For those who choose to help and uplift, the universality of Christ's descent translates into shared heavenly ascent: "My Father sent me that I might be lifted up upon the cross . . . that I might draw all men unto me" (3 Nephi 27:14). Owing to Christ's submission—according to Isaiah he was brought without protest "as a lamb to the slaughter" (Isaiah 53:7)—we are lifted up, if we repent, to share in his exaltation. The divine splendor of that saving moment springs from the depth and steadfastness of Christ's love in the face of unremitting torment and persecution. He broke the bands of death by suffering without thought of malice or vengeance unto death, even as malicious, vengeful men lifted him up to death. Then with that perfect victory secured, Christ became the Mediator between heaven and earth who draws all men unto himself, as he told the Nephites, by offering all people the opportunity to be drawn up unto eternal life should they choose to help and uplift others.

Even those who choose otherwise are lifted up, albeit to be judged unready for eternal life by reason of their refusal to die as to the things of this world so that they might, as Christ said, "bring forth much fruit" in the next world. Having patterned their thinking to a fallen world and believing that it is their one chance to win glory, they are like seeds that will not germinate. They consequently are "hewn down and cast into the fire" (3 Nephi 27:17). Those, however, who, like Nephi, "cry unto the Lord" in prayer and thereby let their hearts be softened by the realization that there is a bigger story in the offing are found "spotless" before God the Father (1 Nephi 2:16; 3 Nephi 27:16, 20). Given their meekness and tractability, their trust-in-God openness to new possibility, they move on to a wider sphere of action involving "eternal lives" (Doctrine and Covenants 132:24).

THE WITNESS OF NATURE

The biological imagery is not accidental. It springs naturally from the agricultural cultures of the Bible and Book of Mormon, and even moderns far removed from farms are not far removed from life-sustaining farm products. Agriculture, of course, is just one of many ways we subjugate nature to our own ends, and while it may be said to be one of our greatest accomplishments, not so nature. By anyone's reckoning, we had nothing to do with its creation, nor with the biological miracles that keep it in creative and procreative process. With this thought in mind, Paul taught that God has revealed himself to all people through the witness of nature: "For the invisible things of him [God] from the creation of the world are clearly seen, being understood by the things that are made [created], even his eternal power and Godhead; so that they are without excuse" (Romans 1:20). We normally do not see God, but we do, as a matter of everyday routine and inescapable fact, experience something cosmically bigger than ourselves. More, that something, while often unpredictable, painful, and destructive, blesses us with food, drink, warmth, shelter, and soul-stretching beauty. The fallen earth is far from perfect, but it clearly resonates overtones of divinity. Those who shrug off its witness while devoting themselves to their own narrow interests are left without excuse, says Paul.

When Paul preached to the Greeks in Athens, he quoted one of their own poets (Aratus) to drive home the point that in God "we live, and move, and have our being" (Acts 17:28). But some of those to whom he preached had already found a way to talk about life and nature without invoking God. The Epicureans, who along with other Greek philosophers took an interest in Paul simply because they had nothing better to do than "either to tell, or to hear some new thing" (v. 21), believed that, owing to their indestructibility, atoms alone were immortal—and also mindless. Departing from traditional cosmology, the Epicureans took pleasure in insisting that there is no divine blueprint. The gods, if they exist, take no interest in human affairs; further, everything ultimately gets zeroed out as mindless atoms, having accidentally achieved human form to fleetingly bring forth life, fall apart to resume their senseless meanderings. Nothing carries over from life to death, because death or lifelessness is the ground state to which everything invariably returns.

This outlook, very much the minority view in antiquity, now strikes many people as eminently reasonable. What other conclusion is possible, some ask, in light of the evil in the world—the wars that appear to have no end, the disasters that senselessly (it seems) befall innocent parties, and the exploitation of animals and children for monetary profit? With so much evil in our midst, it is hard to believe in Providence, particularly when science explains so much and alleviates so much drudgery, even misery, without mention of God.

If Paul could speak to us today, he would, I believe, say that this argument against God is no more persuasive than that offered by the Epicureans; it is, in fact, the same argument, though updated to acknowledge the notable role of science and technology in modern society. If one wishes to start late in the game by shrugging off the witness of nature, then, yes, one can always work up an explanation of things that does not reference any sort of higher power. But this intellectual bubble, Paul would say, is a by-product of God's creation, and like the great and spacious building in Lehi's dream, it floats without foundation and is held temporarily aloft by human presumption. Eventually it will have to come back down to earth, to nature, to the life-giving love that allowed it to spring into existence and that cannot be explained away.

Yes, there is the problem of evil, which problem militates against the proposition of life-giving love, but evil leaps out against a vast backdrop of unremarked, freely offered goodness. God "maketh his sun to rise on the evil and on the good, and sendeth rain on the just and on the unjust" (Matthew 5:45). These are nature metaphors for the all-inclusive love Christ instructs us to adopt: "Love your enemies, bless them that curse you, do good to them that hate you, and pray for them which despitefully use you, and persecute you" (v. 44). From a Christian perspective, love is the universal norm and fount of existence. At the same time, however, it is always under threat of being taken for granted, owing to its ubiquity and sublime impartiality. It is like the air we breathe, or like T. S. Eliot's music, which is "heard so deeply that it is not heard at all."[7]

To be sure, hate-inspired evil exists, but it looms all the larger when we pick it out exclusively while failing to realize that it is thrown into relief by the goodness that prevails in nature, which goodness points back to God. Mindless atoms could not have produced the present universe with all its instances of harmony and beauty, nor could they have haphazardly collected together to form beings with powers of thought, feeling, and imagination wholly absent in the atoms themselves. Here again we have entities floating without foundation, this time living beings whipped up out of a void of lifelessness. For Paul nothing made less sense. Such thinking was possible only because we live in a universe quickened by divine love. The very reason we can stray into such errant byways is because God opened an expanse in which we could "live, and move, and have our being."

More than that, evil does not count as evidence against God, because its baleful effects may be subordinated to divine ends. Without evil, Lehi taught, we could not know goodness; without misery, we could not know joy. But the gospel motif of opposition in all things does not imply equality of opposites; rather, it points back to a loving God able to bring evil into the orbit of good so that the two can mix together for a higher purpose. The nature of evil is to brood narcissistically on perceived injustices, to accuse others "day and night" as Lucifer did (Revelation 12:10), and to shut them out. God's nature is to lovingly include others, to draw them in and then, should they repent, draw them up to eternal life. It is this love that turns existence into a "compound in one" because it overleaps polarizing differences. And in virtue of this magnificent act of divine outreach, God is able to turn evil toward good ends so that its hurt reregisters as happiness. "The sting of death is sin," wrote Paul, but "thanks be to God, which giveth us the victory [over death] through our Lord Jesus Christ," we now have reason to rejoice (1 Corinthians 15:56–57).

"Where danger is also grows the saving power," wrote the poet-philosopher Friedrich Hölderlin.[8] Without peril and tribulation, salvation would be a meaningless affair, for there would be nothing to be saved from; and we, if it could be said that we existed at all, would be none the wiser, living in a flat world with no opposition. Thanks be to God, though, we live in a deeply textured, deeply tensioned, multivalent world that stretches us "wide as eternity" (Moses 7:41). First but not necessarily foremost, we live, as Paul said, under the "bondage of corruption" (Romans 8:21), enchained to our fallen mortal bodies and to a fallen ephemeral world where "earth's joys grow dim, its glories pass away."[9] But though we are intimate with our fallen condition, we are not completely at home with it. "Oh as I was young and easy in the mercy of his means, / Time held me green and dying / Though I sang in my chains like the sea," wrote the Welsh poet Dylan Thomas.[10] We sing in our chains like the sea against our mortality, and our strivings on earth spring from our desire to find "a city which hath foundations [rather than airy intellectual props], whose builder and maker is God" (Hebrews 11:10). Or as Saint Augustine, the preeminent fifth-century theologian, wrote, addressing God in prayer: "Our hearts are restless until they find their rest in you."[11]

Another reason evil does not count as evidence against God is that we know in the restlessness of our hearts that the "bondage of corruption" is not the end of the story. This is not wishful thinking but a consequence of the fact that if absolute evil or meaninglessness were the sum of existence, the question of meaning, and of God's existence, would never arise. If darkness were everything, no one would wish it away, for the possibility of light—a nonexistent entity—would never register. "Birds do not sing in caves," wrote Thoreau, but in places where the light-dark rhythms of nature give them something to sing about.[12] Our struggle against mortal frailty, and "against the rulers of the darkness of this world [and] spiritual wickedness in high places" (Ephesians 6:12), signifies light and goodness, rays of which counterbalance darkness and spark our quest for greater light and goodness.

THE PROMISE OF NATURE

Paul wants us to realize that Epicurean-like denials of divinity would be impossible if God did not exist. In recent centuries, unfortunately, this attitude of denial has so naturalized Western thought as to go virtually unchallenged, the result being that what was once regarded as an open question is now for many people a settled issue. What, we may ask, has happened to reorient our thinking toward the Epicurean belief that lifelessness is the cosmic default state?

The question has inspired much research. Here I offer a brief two-paragraph summary that should make sense to anyone even remotely familiar with scientific assumptions about nature. We begin with Johannes Kepler, who in about 1600 declared that he had decided to quit thinking of the cosmos as a divine organism so that he could begin thinking of it as a mechanical clock—the most compelling machine of his era.[13] Living at a tipping point in Western thought, Kepler appreciated the epistemic value of the clock metaphor: a mechanical universe would be much easier to explain than one informed by living powers, some of them divine. While Kepler did not believe in atoms, and though his science was steeped in religious belief, he was also partial to the Epicurean proposition that physical reality could be reduced to mechanical principles.

Kepler's success in effecting this reduction, coupled with the success of Galileo, Descartes, Newton, and others, was so persuasive that later thinkers argued that physical reality is exhaustive of all reality. When asked by Napoleon Bonaparte regarding the role of God in his scientific world picture, the great scientist Pierre-Simon Laplace famously responded, "I have no need of that hypothesis."[14] This proposition—that one can fully explain reality without referencing spiritual (nonphysical) agencies—became a bandwagon on which many others would climb, and soon it would become an article of faith in Western thought—"the definitive explanatory principle of all events."[15] Science still subscribes to it today, along with the notion of mindless atoms the Epicureans had claimed were the basis of all reality, though, of course, the modern understanding of atoms (and subatomic particles) is much more subtle and complex.

Suffice it to say, if mindless atoms of any complexity are assumed to be the basis of all reality, then lifelessness becomes the unchallenged rule and life the anomalous and difficult-to-explain exception to the rule. This is the present state of affairs in modern scientific thought, but it is exactly upside-down compared to Paul's teaching. For him physical death was not reversion to the rule of lifelessness but, as the seasonal round of nature demonstrates, a leave-taking from mortality so that rebirth and resurrection might occur at a higher plane. Echoing Christ, he taught that seeds cannot be quickened or raised to new life unless they first die: "But some man will say, How are the dead raised up? and with what body do they come? Thou fool, that which thou sowest is not quickened, except it die" (1 Corinthians 15:35–36).

Paul is proposing that mortality is a time when our frail, imperfect bodies break down and fall into the earth like seeds in order to be born anew, this time whole, perfected, and glorified: the resurrection of the dead, though "sown in corruption," is "raised in incorruption"; though sown in dishonor and weakness, is raised in glory and power (1 Corinthians 15:42–43). Using similar organic imagery, Brigham Young remarked on the same upward-spiraling, dying-and-quickening process:

> Our bodies are all important to us, though they may be old and withered, emaciated with toil, pain, and sickness, and our limbs bent with rheumatism, all uniting to hasten dissolution, for death is sown in our mortal bodies. The food and drink we partake of are contaminated with the seeds of death, yet we partake of them to extend our lives until our allotted work is finished, when our tabernacles, in a state of ripeness, are sown in the earth to produce immortal fruit.[16]

This view of the Resurrection dovetails with Paul's belief that nature testifies of God's reality and goodness. Further, that testimony does not require deep study, because it is always on display. A seed begins to grow by "dying," that is, by giving up most of its substance to nourish the germ within it. This small gift initiates a process that eventually produces, when compared to the originally sown seed, a galaxy of life: many seeds germinating as plants proliferate to produce new seeds and plants as far as the imagination can reach. This is the arithmetic of life, and for Paul it was an image of Christ's sacrificial death and the all-inclusive, ever-expanding newness of life that flows therefrom.

If the imagery seems a little off—a little too organic maybe—that is not surprising. Later Christians found Paul's language too redolent of natural processes and undertook to recharacterize the Resurrection as an inorganic event similar to the repair of broken pottery or the restoration of old and torn clothing.[17] Thus "inorganic pictures of the resurrected body ... [were] grafted uneasily onto Paul's organic imagery."[18] Neither image is wrong, but the latter tracks back to the flora of the natural world, their spontaneous efflorescence from tiny, seemingly nondescript beginnings (seeds). A similar efflorescence occurs during the resurrection of the dead, Paul taught, though at a higher turn of the salvific spiral, and this is because, thanks be to God, Christ's triumph over death is, as nature so vibrantly demonstrates, life-quickening.

Thus the living witness of nature is also a promise of new life, and, according to Paul, a promise whose fulfillment nature yearns and lives for. If in the restlessness of our hearts we "groan within ourselves, waiting for the adoption, to wit, the redemption of our body," so also does "the whole creation," writes Paul (Romans 8:22–23). In a parallel passage from the Book of Moses, Enoch hears the earth cry for relief from the evil that prevails upon it: "When shall I rest, and be cleansed from the filthiness which is gone forth out of me? When will my Creator sanctify me, that I may rest, and righteousness for a season abide upon my face?" (Moses 7:48).

One may understand these passages as the personification of lifeless elements, but pioneer Latter-day Saints were open to the view that a sentient earth feelingly shares our destiny. The earth, Brigham Young taught, fell from grace "to pass through certain ordeals, together with the people on it."[19] And to assist in our exaltation. According to Apostle George A. Smith, "the elements, including the water, the soil and all that surround them, are actually aching for the brethren to combine them together and make . . . choice productions of a mild climate; all these elements are ready to render aid to build up Zion."[20] Making the same point, Heber C. Kimball, a counselor in the Church's First Presidency, asked: "How does the earth feel, when righteous men and women are walking upon it, ploughing it, hoeing it, watering it, blessing it! I will tell you the earth feels it, and every part of the earth that is attached to it."[21] Finally, Daniel H. Wells, also a counselor in the First Presidency, insisted that the "man who . . . plants a single fruit tree . . . and cultivates it, and cause[s] it to bring forth more fruit, he has done something towards his exaltation—has made one step towards redeeming the earth from sin . . . and from the curse pronounced against it."[22]

Such statements function as a litmus test to reveal one's attitude toward nature. If we tend to shrug them off as wishful sentimentality, the Epicurean thesis of elemental lifelessness may be governing our thinking. We may be assuming that lifelessness is the cosmic default condition, and so rocks, mountains, planets, and perhaps even flora and fauna lack the capacity to yearn for redemption and the glorious transformation that occasions the promise of "a new heaven and a new earth" (Revelation 21:1). Said differently, our supposition may be that nature is, at bottom, lifeless and therefore oblivious to the drama of salvation being played on its stage. Whatever harmony nature displays, therefore, occurs mindlessly—that is, accidentally and aimlessly—and not, as Paul proposed, in praise and witness of the Creator.

The salient difference between the two outlooks reduces to the question of whether God's love washes over the entire cosmos, running into every nook and cranny and inflecting reality at every level with grace and life, or whether his love stops short at some point—perhaps at so-called inanimate matter consisting of lifeless atoms. Is physical creation, with all the terror, pain, joy, and beauty it brings to us, the heartfelt though fallen handiwork of God, or is it only partly lit up by God's love and therefore only partly transfigured by his creative, quickening touch? In brief, does the universe—the cosmos organized out of primeval material—instantiate God's love, or do we find that love flourishing only in tiny pockets here and there in contravention to the great rule of lifelessness that otherwise controls physical reality?

For Paul the universe marks the "the breadth, and length, and depth, and height" (Ephesians 3:18) of God's love because Jesus has secured the universal victory of life over death in our behalf. We live within the cosmic embrace of God's love, though that embrace does not, as we might wish, situate us in an Edenic garden absent of challenge and opposition. Rather, it locates us smack-dab in the middle of a compound-in-one existence where evil and pain may be seen as evidence against God and lifelessness may be deemed the cosmic ground state. These sensibilities are just two of the many prerogatives God's love affords us, but if either was absolutely true there would be no tension in the

THE WITNESS AND PROMISE OF NATURE

world to alert us to that fact. As Lehi wrote, there would be "no creation" and we would not exist as agents able to think and act for ourselves (2 Nephi 2:13).

Although Albert Einstein did not believe in a God who takes an interest in one's personal affairs, his science was religiously motivated in the sense that the cosmos offered an escape from "the narrow whirlpool of personal experience" and the "painful crudity and hopeless dreariness" of everyday life.[23] With nothing to draw us outward and upward, everyday life would indeed be dreary to the point of futility. Nature, however, is one means whereby that soul-stretching function is accomplished, and it restates the love of God even when we choose to believe otherwise. If nature is without rhyme or reason, as some thinkers insist, how then does it spark our interest and inspire hope of greater understanding? If, in fact, it is "a tale told by an idiot, full of sound and fury, signifying nothing,"[24] how does it invite us into its inner precincts and bless us with a sense of intellectual and even spiritual adventure? Like many others who did not believe in a loving, saving God, Einstein nevertheless responded to the promise of salvation that nature embodies: "Out yonder there was this huge world, which exists independently of us human beings and which stands before us like a great, eternal riddle, at least partially accessible to our inspection and thinking. The contemplation of this world beckoned like a liberation."[25]

Paul would say that because God fulfills his promises in ways that break the frame of mortal understanding, the promise of liberation that motivated Einstein's science spills over into the next world. Nature, though wondrous, is more promise of arrival than arrival, more suggestion than substance, more uplift and intimation than ultimate realization. "What's a heaven for," asked the Victorian poet Robert

Browning, if it cannot inspire an upward reach?[26] Nature, though fallen, reaches upward, just as we do.

NOTES

1. Francesca Fremantle, *Luminous Emptiness: Understanding the Tibetan Book of the Dead* (Boston: Shambhala, 2001), 13.
2. M. Russell Ballard, "'This Is My Work and Glory,'" *Ensign*, May 2013.
3. Brigham Young, in *Journal of Discourses*, 26 vols. (London: Latter-day Saints' Book Depot, 1854–86), 9:288.
4. Brigham Young, in *Journal of Discourses*, 17:142.
5. I cite this version because it spells out the implications of futurity associated with *earnest*, the slightly obsolete word used in the King James Version.
6. Brigham Young, in *Journal of Discourses*, 6:333.
7. T. S. Eliot, "The Dry Salvages," in *The Complete Poems and Plays: 1909–1950* (New York: Harcourt, Brace, and World, 1952), 130–37.
8. From the opening lines of his poem "Patmos," translated from the original German.
9. Henry F. Lyte, "Abide with Me," http://library.timelesstruths.org/music/Abide_with_Me/.
10. Dylan Thomas, "Fern Hill," https://www.poets.org/poetsorg/poem/fern-hill.
11. *St. Augustine's Confessions*, book I, chapter 1.
12. Henry David Thoreau, *Walden, or, Life in the Woods* (Garden City, NY: Anchor, 1973), 28.
13. See letter to Herwart von Hohenberg, Catholic Chancellor of Bavaria, February 10, 1605; quoted in Alfred W. Crosby, *The Measure of Reality: Quantification and Western Society: 1250–1600* (Cambridge: Cambridge University Press, 1997), 84.
14. Quoted in *Routledge Encyclopedia of Philosophy*, ed. Edward Craig (New York: Routledge, 1998), 6:172.
15. *Routledge Encyclopedia of Philosophy*, 6:172.
16. Brigham Young, in *Journal of Discourses*, 9:288.
17. "The seed is the oldest Christian metaphor for the resurrection of the body," writes Caroline Walker Bynum. "It is the dominant

THE WITNESS AND PROMISE OF NATURE

metaphor in that text which, more than any other, has determined discussion of resurrection. . . . The seed of I Corinthians 15 grows: as 'bare' grain it dies in the ground, then quickens to new life in a new body." Caroline Walker Bynum, *The Resurrection of the Body in Western Christianity, 200–1336* (New York: Columbia University, 1995), 3.

18. Sanjeev Nagar, *Fundamentals of Christianity* (New Delhi: Mahaveer and Sons, 2010), loc. 1619, Kindle.
19. Brigham Young, in *Journal of Discourses*, 8:297. This paragraph is drawn from my article "Heaven-Earth Wedges: The Mormon Experience," *Proteus: A Journal of Ideas* 15, no. 2 (Fall 1998): 59–65.
20. George A. Smith, in *Journal of Discourses*, 10:122.
21. Heber C. Kimball, in *Journal of Discourses*, 6:133.
22. Daniel H. Wells, in *Journal of Discourses*, 9:363.
23. Albert Einstein, "Principles of Research," 1918 address given on the occasion of Max Planck's sixtieth birthday, http://www.site.uottawa.ca/~yymao/misc/Einstein_PlanckBirthday.html.
24. William Shakespeare, *Macbeth*, act 5, scene 5.
25. Albert Einstein, "Autobiographical Notes," in *Albert Einstein; Philosopher-Scientist*, ed. Paul Arthur Schilpp (La Salle, IL: Open Court, 1991), 5.
26. Robert Browning, "Andrea del Sarto," http://www.poetryfoundation.org/poem/173001.

CHAPTER 5

Receiving All Things with Thanksgiving

I am startled that God can make me so rich even with my own cheap stores.
—Henry David Thoreau

The unthankful heart . . . discovers no mercies; but let the thankful heart sweep through the day and, as the magnet finds the iron, so it will find, in every hour, some heavenly blessings.
—Henry Ward Beecher

Gratitude unlocks the fullness of life. It turns what we have into enough, and more. It turns denial into acceptance, chaos to order, confusion to clarity. It can turn a meal into a feast, a house into home, a stranger into a friend.
—Melody Beattie, *The Language of Letting Go*

In his epistles Paul insisted that those who have tasted the love of God are privy to an experience that cannot be grasped from the outside. To the Saints at Corinth he wrote, "Eye hath not seen, nor ear heard, neither have entered into the heart of man, the things which God hath prepared for them that love him" (1 Corinthians 2:9).

Centuries later Bernard of Clairvaux, a Cistercian monk and advisor to five popes, memorialized this truth in verse:

> Jesus, the very thought of thee
> with sweetness fills the breast;
> but sweeter far thy face to see,
> and in thy presence rest.
>
> O hope of every contrite heart,
> O joy of all the meek,
> to those who fall, how kind thou art!
> How good to those who seek!
>
> But what to those who find? Ah, this
> nor tongue nor pen can show;
> the love of Jesus, what it is,
> none but his loved ones know.[1]

To know God's love as revealed through his Son is the crowning experience of life, according to Bernard and Paul. But to call it the "crowning experience" is to class it with lesser experience, and this diminishes it. What Paul at least had in mind was an experience that imparts light and meaning to every other experience, much as the sun imparts light to the earth. The visual splendor of terrestrial nature is not self-originating; it is announced by the sun, and thanks also to the sun that physically supports us from moment to moment, we are alive to witness that splendor. Analogously, the love of God is intrinsic to the makeup of the cosmos, according to Paul, and when we apprehend this truth, our everyday experiences suddenly catch fire in ways previously unimaginable. To those standing on the outside and viewing events with a critical eye, though, nothing changes. That, however, is just the point: "The love of Jesus, what it is, / none but his loved ones know."

"In the glowing hour of excitement," wrote the noted philosopher and psychologist William James in his discussion of religious conversion, "all incomprehensibilities are solved, and what was so enigmatical from without becomes transparently obvious. Each emotion obeys a logic of its own, and makes deductions which no other logic can draw. Piety and charity live in a different universe from worldly lusts and fears, and form another centre of energy altogether."[2] I would add that along with piety and charity, gratitude lives in not just a different universe from worldly wants and insecurities, but one vastly larger.

THE FULLNESS OF THE EARTH IS YOURS

A subtext here is that the meek shall inherit the earth. Those who are humble enough to feel small and reverential amid the wonders of the physical creation are given co-ownership of the cosmos, albeit by means of divine understanding that elevates the "least thing," whether a grain of sand, a fallen sparrow, or a humble servant of the Lord, to a level of profound worth. Unfortunately, however, our minds are habitually blinkered by zero-sum, legalistic thought: if I possess this plot of ground, you cannot, and here are the legal documents that establish my claim. As binding as such claims of legal entitlement may feel, they are rendered null and void by our inability to create what we profess to own. Merely having found ourselves on a planet of surpassing beauty, we have incongruously laid claim to it as if it sprang from our hard work and genius. But, of course, the pristine earth is no more our handiwork than are the stars, though, unlike the stars, it is within our reach and therefore subject to our exploitation should we come to see it merely as an economic resource. The pity is that if we do see it that way, our vision of all else is similarly tainted. When looking up at the stars, Cecil Rhodes, who made his fortune mining diamonds in South Africa, did not feel to praise God; rather he was chagrined because he could not get at them, could not impose his entrepreneurial will on them. "The world is nearly all parcelled out," he stated, "and what there is left of it is being divided up, conquered, and colonised. To think of these stars that you see overhead at night, these vast worlds which we can never reach. I would annex the planets if I could; I often think of that. It makes me sad to see them so clear and yet so far."[3]

The restored gospel counteracts such thinking by replacing the idea of private ownership with that of stewardship. "You own nothing," declared Brigham Young, "I own nothing. . . . The Lord has placed what I have in my hands, to see what I will do with it, and I am perfectly willing for Him to dispose of it otherwise whenever he pleases."[4] Indeed, "not one particle of all that comprises this vast creation of God is our own. Everything we have has been bestowed upon us for our action, to see what we would do with it—whether we would use it for eternal life and exaltation or for eternal death and degradation."[5] Paradoxically, upon meekly acknowledging the Lord as the rightful owner and giver of all that we legally possess, we vastly enlarge our capacity to enjoy other things. Here two truths touch together: (1) "The earth is the Lord's, and the fullness thereof" (Psalm 24:1); and (2) God is a giver of "good" and "perfect gift[s]" (James 1:17)—he is, as Joseph Smith said, "more liberal in his views, and boundless in his mercies and blessings, than we are ready to believe or receive."[6]

God delights in blessing his children; he delights in sharing his creation with them, but of course such sharing cannot occur if, feeling no dependence on God, they see the earth as something to be divided up, conquered, and colonized. Such is one way of owning the earth, but the other, more joyful way coincides with Henry David Thoreau's observation that ownership of the earth consists not in property records but in one's capacity to drink in the beauty of nature.[7] Thereby is the Lord's aim "to please the eye and to gladden the heart" satisfied against the backdrop of his pronouncement that "the fulness of the earth is yours" (see Doctrine and Covenants 59:16–18). We own the earth and cosmos already if we are humble enough to receive them with thanksgiving, a glad heart, and a cheerful countenance (v. 15). These virtues answer to the selfless, noncompetitive sharing of the universe that the gospel encourages and that in fact the universe affords: a sharing that is win-win, mutually edifying, and bound up in the everyday realization that we best enjoy the wonders of creation in the company of others. When we go sightseeing, we like to take others along.

To be sure, if we assume that nature's offerings are too thinly spread among too many people, then our picture of the world, and our everyday behavior, will follow suit. But this characterization runs counter to the Lord's declaration that "the earth is full, and there is enough and to spare" (Doctrine and Covenants 104:17). That is, full of the kinds of natural resources that the Lord delights to share with his children, as when "the hand of providence . . . smiled . . . most pleasingly" upon Jacob's people, enabling them to "obtain many riches" (Jacob 2:13). For the Nephites the problem was never one of too few resources, but rather that some people managed to accumulate and hold on to those resources more successfully than others, which inequality led to pride, social stratification, and the persecution of those less wealthy.

If this is the path we choose, to let every person prosper "according to his [own] genius," as Korihor put it (Alma 30:17), we miss out on real happiness even when we do prosper. We miss out because we implement the wrong formula of ownership, one based on an incorrect understanding of physical reality. The universe is not a vast repository of goods waiting to be divided up, conquered, and colonized, but an expression of God's love. It embodies God's desire to share with his children his more abundant life—a life in which blessings snowball as they are shared and reshared with others.

This is the larger way of sharing spoken of in the scriptures and the way that motivates (or should motivate) all charitable giving. We believe that what we give to others is not just dribbled away until it no longer makes a difference; rather, God multiplies it toward ends larger than we envision. What we give, we ultimately give back to God, and he gathers our gifts into his work and his glory, which is to "bring to pass the immortality and eternal life of man" (Moses 1:39). Thus our acts of kindness circle back to bless us, having first circulated into the cosmic economy of God's love.

OVERSTEPPING OUR MORTAL CONFINEMENT

That economy is on offer everywhere we look, although for most of us it has been iterated out of sight through deep familiarity. We are like fish that cannot take cognizance of the water that supports their movement and enables their oxygen intake. It is hard for us to see the ambient love of God whereby, as Paul said, we "live, and move, and have our being" (Acts 17:28). All the same, it is right in front of us, at each moment reminding us—if we let it—that there is a bigger story in the offing than the one that now seems to delimit us. If we are looking for a physical sign of what God has in mind for us, all we need do is look skyward. There we may see the stars announcing God's promise of eternal posterity to Abraham and his seed. Or on a clear day, as the song says, we may see "forever"—an unending expanse suggesting unending life, according to the celebrated twentieth-century philosopher Ludwig Wittgenstein: "Our life has no end in just the way in which our visual field has no limits."[8]

Some may dismiss this as wishful thinking, but only because they fail to grasp the proposition in all its bearings. Wittgenstein is remarking on the amazing fact that we are visually participatory in the vast cosmos despite the spatial and temporal limitations of the mortal experience. We lead an earthbound life for perhaps eighty years, but we escape the physical confinement of our mortal bodies as our perceptual faculties gather in the universe. Despite our mortal frailty and the body's tendency to self-implode, we are in many ways turned outward and are thereby attuned to rhythms that vastly exceed our brief stay on earth. Without this attunement, this consonance with the larger world, our perceptual experience would be confined to bodily function and whatever inner experience we might imaginatively muster up. Our lives, in brief, would be stunted and completely narcissistic, nipped in the bud before they were allowed to blossom, although not knowing anything different, we would not be the wiser.

While we often marvel at the universe and see it as evidence of God's existence, no less remarkable, and no less indicative of God's goodness, is our ability to drink in the majesty and beauty of God's creation. Thereby we see through "a glass, darkly" (1 Corinthians 13:12), a fact that suggests we are already partway home to God, for if Satan had his way, our existence would be fully shut up and cave-like. Instead it is partly given over to the possibility that we are destined for things larger than we know. Through the perceptual openings in our bodies, we peer in wonder at an unbounded world; indeed, we expansively mingle into that world, although so elemental is this aspect of our being that only poets seem to remember it. To follow Emily Dickinson:

> The brain is wider than the sky,
> For, put them side by side,
> The one the other will include
> With ease, and you beside.[9]

And Wallace Stevens:

> I measure myself
> Against a tall tree.
> I find that I am much taller,
> For I reach right up to the sun,
> With my eye.[10]

And this is just the start, the seeing darkly through our imperfect perceptual faculties. But it is enough to establish the readily forgotten point that we are cosmically wide-open beings, although, to be sure, we are heavily laden with mundane needs and proclivities. Amphibious beings, we are blessed to live in two realms, which in fact are "a compound in one": the hardscrabble, earthbound world of our bodily needs and the soul-stretching upper reaches of spirit, imagination, and perceptual experience. While the former realm is all about restraint and limitation, the latter prefigures ongoing, open-ended expansion—our gradual deliverance from dark seeing by means of light that "groweth brighter and brighter until the perfect day" (Doctrine and Covenants 50:24).

"If the doors of perception were cleansed," wrote the English Romantic poet William Blake, "everything would appear to man as it is, Infinite."[11] Our mortal weakness obscures our embryonic immortality; the "infinite [is hidden up] in the finite, the more in the less," as the French philosopher Emmanuel Levinas remarked,[12] where it is hard to see and, when seen, generally rejected as inferior. According to Isaiah, the mortal Christ would have "no form nor comeliness; . . . no beauty that we should desire him" (Isaiah 53:2). He was the stone rejected by the builders of the temple (see Matthew 21:42; Acts 4:11). He came as a lowly servant, wrote Paul, "ma[king] himself of no reputation" and suffering an ignominious death, though he was "in the form of God" (see Philippians 2:6–8). He cast his lot with the poor, the outcast, the despised, the "least of these my brethren" (Matthew 25:40).

But except for his willing descent "below all things," Christ could not have ascended "above all things" (Doctrine and Covenants 88:6, 42). His abasement was the precondition for his resurrection and ascension into heaven. We undergo a similar passage, though ours is far less demanding because we enjoy the blessings that sprang into existence once he opened a path out of darkness. The wide-open world restates that opening. When we look up at the stars and planets, we see God "moving in his majesty and power" (v. 47). Or, during the day, we may see nothing but endless expanse, suggestive of eternal life. Even when we look at specific objects, we see things that "bear record" of God (Moses 6:63) and always with the sense that there is yet more to be seen.[13] Further, when we receive these things with joyful appreciation, we enter with amazement into the Lord's delight. "But were it told me, Today, / That I might have the Sky" and its myriad contents, wrote Emily Dickinson, "my Heart / Would split" and "The news would strike me dead." And yet before she goes back behind her windowpane of conventional thought, she exults in what she sees:

> The Meadows—mine—
> The Mountains—mine—
> All Forests—Stintless stars—
> As much of noon, as I could take—
> Between my finite eyes—
>
> The Motions of the Dipping Birds—
> The Morning's Amber Road—
> ....[14]

This, however, is not the end, nor even the beginning, of God's generosity to his children as he lets them drink in his handiwork. The following fact is so close to home that it may never register: In our elemental viewing of nature we do not jostle or compete with each other for a place at the table. My wide consciousness of the world does not interfere with yours. William James made this point in an article entitled "Human Immortality":

> Each new mind brings its own edition of the universe of space along with it, its own room to inhabit; and these spaces never crowd each other,—the space of my imagination, for example, in no way interferes with yours. The amount of possible consciousness seems to be governed by no law analogous to that of the so-called conservation of energy in the material world. When one man wakes up, or one is born, another does not have to go to sleep, or die, in

order to keep the consciousness of the universe a constant quantity.[15]

If we let each "edition of the universe" count as a universe, we find ourselves in a multiverse where universes freely coexist and interpenetrate. And as James points out, this multiverse (unlike the entropic universe given us by science) is not a zero-sum system regulated by space-time constraints and energy conservation laws. We will never have to worry about an overproliferation of consciousness. It seems that in this respect—the way my consciousness of reality does not compete with or crowd out yours—we already live in a wide-open world suggestive of heaven. That is, one that prefigures God's promise that all that he has will be ours (see Doctrine and Covenants 84:38).

COMING BACK TO GRATITUDE

The key, as noted earlier, is to receive God's creation with gladness and thanksgiving, a way of life that prepares us for the celestial kingdom, wherein all things are had in common (see Doctrine and Covenants 78:6–7). The earth and its fullness cannot be enjoyed in any other way, for it embodies the Lord's delight in blessing his children. His love is "water springing up into everlasting life" (John 4:14). It cannot be bottled, monopolized, or commodified, but must by its own nature overflow—freely, spontaneously, "without compulsory means" (Doctrine and Covenants 121:46). The difficulty is that we lose sight of God's wondrous love as it spills into the world around us and eventually see everything by "the light of common day."[16] Our sense of awe atrophies as we grow into the zero-sum practices of human culture.

Helen Keller's experience is instructive in this regard. Having lost her sight and hearing in early infancy, she was able to drink in very little of the world's meaning until Anne Sullivan found a way to transmit it by code. Then by the miracle of language the world exploded into being. Rehearsing the experience, Keller wrote:

> We walked down the path to the well-house, attracted by the fragrance of the honeysuckle with which it was covered. Someone was drawing water and my teacher placed my hand under the spout. As the cool stream gushed over one hand she spelled into the other the word "water," first slowly, then rapidly. I stood still, my whole attention fixed upon the motion of her fingers. Suddenly I felt a misty consciousness as of something forgotten—a thrill of returning thought; and somehow the mystery of language was revealed to me. I knew then that "w-a-t-e-r" meant the wonderful cool something that was flowing over my hand. That living word awakened my soul, gave it light, joy, set it free! . . . I left the well-house eager to learn. Everything had a name, and each name gave birth to a new thought. As we returned to the house each object that I touched seemed to quiver with life. That was because I saw everything with the strange new light that had come to me.[17]

Elsewhere she recalled that the "word 'water' dropped into my mind like the sun in a frozen winter world."[18] Helen may have been blind and deaf in a medical sense, but her sudden apprehension of a larger world full of signs and meanings was astonishingly vivid. She received the experience as a divine gift and came to regard her blindness and deafness as blessings that helped her hang on to that gift:

> To one who is deaf and blind the spiritual world offers no difficulty. . . . I am often conscious of beautiful flowers and

birds and laughing children where to my seeing associates there is nothing. They skeptically declare that I see "light that never was on sea or land." But I know that their mystic sense is dormant, and that is why there are so many barren places in their lives. They prefer "facts" to vision.[19]

As Helen uses the words, *vision* refers to awakening or birth, while *facts* refers to propositions cut off from the wonder of their birth. Because her awakening occurred relatively late in life, she was able to hang on to it more successfully than most people do. Like the blinded Gloucester, she saw the world "feelingly" while feeling her way from one marvel to the next.[20] She remembered the sudden expansion of light that accompanied her entry into the world of sociality, communication, art, and science, while her friends merely attended to that world itself, missing the life-awakening "light that never was on sea or land." They, in her judgment, had forgotten the world-giving miracle, and as a result their sense of wonder had grown dim. They had, as William Wordsworth put it, transitioned from an early childhood when all the world seemed "apparell'd in celestial light" to a long adulthood marked by "the light of common day." Perhaps they had, to follow T. S. Eliot, simply grown tired of so much ecstatic radiance: "In our rhythm of earthly life we tire of light. We are glad when the day ends, when the play ends; and ecstasy is too much pain."[21]

Christ is "the true light that lighteth every man that cometh into the world" (Doctrine and Covenants 93:2). That light reveals the wonder of his love as we drink in the vast, magnificent universe from our tiny, earthbound vantage points. Of course, the revelation, the vision, dims if we do not receive it with joy and thanksgiving. But if we do, we become joint-heirs with Christ, receiving all that he possesses within an economy of love where possessions multiply as they are shared.

This way of gathering up goods is so alien to our normal practice that the Lord patiently waits for us to put our trust in his arm: "Verily, verily, I say unto you, ye are little children, and ye have not as yet understood how great blessings the Father hath in his own hands and prepared for you." Further, he acknowledges our weakness but mercifully allows for it, all the while reminding us that there is no cause for despair: "And ye cannot bear all things now; nevertheless, be of good cheer, for I will lead you along. The kingdom is yours and the blessings thereof are yours, and the riches of eternity are yours." Finally, the Lord admonishes us to gratitude, for gratitude catalyzes the multiplication miracle that sweeps us into eternal life: "And he who receiveth all things with thankfulness shall be made glorious; and the things of this earth shall be added unto him, even an hundred fold, yea, more" (Doctrine and Covenants 78:17–19).

Not that we aspire to expand our personal sway and dominion, but that we are "added unto" as our everyday thinking and conduct begin to hum the miracles of God's love, one of which is that there is no bottom to that love. Those who pledge themselves to Christ, therefore, will receive an "everlasting dominion" that shall spring up "without compulsory means . . . forever and ever" (Doctrine and Covenants 121:46). And not just in the next world, but already in this world as heaven gently maps itself onto mortality. Thus all the way to heaven is heaven.

NOTES

1. Bernard of Clairvaux, "Jesus, the Very Thought of Thee," *United Methodist Hymnal* (1989), https://hymnary.org/text/jesus_the_very_thought_of_thee.
2. William James, *The Varieties of Religious Experience* (New York: Barnes and Noble Classics, 2004), 286.
3. Quoted in *The Last Will and Testament of Cecil John Rhodes*, ed. W. T. Stead (London: William Clowes and Sons, 1902), 190.
4. Brigham Young, in *Journal of Discourses*, 26 vols. (London: Latter-day Saints' Book Depot, 1854–86), 10:298.
5. Brigham Young, in *Journal of Discourses*, 8:67.
6. Joseph Smith, History, 1838–1856, volume D-1 [1 August 1842–1 July 1843] [addenda], p. 4 [addenda], http://josephsmithpapers.org/.
7. Henry David Thoreau, *Walden, or, Life in the Woods* (Garden City, NY: Anchor, 1973), 72–73. After nearly buying a piece of property, whose owner changed his mind at the last minute and offered to pay a ten-dollar fee for reneging on the transaction, Thoreau remarked that he had refused the fee. He then wrote: "I found thus that I had been a rich man without any damage to my poverty. But I retained the landscape, and I have since annually carried off what it yielded without a wheelbarrow. . . . I have frequently seen a poet withdraw, having enjoyed the most valuable part of a farm, while the crusty farmer supposed that he had got a few wild apples only. Why, the owner does not know it for many years when a poet has put his farm in rhyme, the most admirable kind of invisible fence, has fairly impounded it, milked it, skimmed it, and got all the cream, and left the farmer only the skimmed milk."
8. Ludwig Wittgenstein, *Tractatus Logico-Philosophicus*, 6:4311, trans. D. F. Pears and B. F. McGuinness (London: Routledge, 2001), 87. The song "On a Clear Day (You Can See Forever)" is from a 1965 musical with the same title.
9. Emily Dickinson, "The brain is wider than the sky," *Selected Poems* (New York: Gramercy, 1993), 24.
10. Wallace Stevens, "Six Significant Landscapes," in *The Collected Poems of Wallace Stevens* (New York: Alfred A. Knopf, 1968), 74.

11. William Blake, *The Marriage of Heaven and Hell*, in *The Portable Blake*, ed. Alfred Kazin (New York: Viking Press, 1972), 258.
12. Emmanuel Levinas, *Totality and Infinity*, trans. Alphonso Lingis (Pittsburgh: Duquesne University Press, 1969), 50.
13. See Maurice Merleau-Ponty, *Phenomenology of Perception*, trans. M. Colin Smith (London: Routledge and Kegan Paul, 1962), 67–68. See my article "Merleau-Ponty's Visual Space and the Law of Large Numbers," *Studia Phænomenologica* 6 (2006): 391–406.
14. Emily Dickinson, "Before I got my eye put out," https://www.poetryfoundation.org/poems/52135/before-i-got-my-eye-put-out-336.
15. William James, "Human Immortality," in *William James: Writings, 1878–1899*, ed. Gerald E. Myers (New York: Library of America, 1992), 1125.
16. William Wordsworth, "Ode: Intimations of Immortality from Recollections of Early Childhood," in *Oxford Book of English Verse, 1250–1900*, ed. Arthur Quiller-Couch (Oxford: Clarendon, 1912), 612.
17. Helen Keller, *The Story of My Life* (London: Hodder and Stoughton, 1959), 23; quoted by Henri Bortoft in *The Wholeness of Nature: Goethe's Way toward a Science of Conscious Participation in Nature* (Hudson, NY: Lindisfarne, 1996), 312.
18. Helen Keller, *My Religion* (New York: Swedenborg Foundation, 1960), 153–54.
19. Keller, *My Religion*, 157; spelling modernized.
20. William Shakespeare, *King Lear*, act 4, scene 6.
21. T. S. Eliot, "Choruses from 'The Rock,'" in *T. S. Eliot: The Complete Poems and Plays, 1909–1950* (New York: Harcourt, Brace and World), 112.

Index

A

Abraham
    cosmological vision of, 23
    journey of, x, 22
Abrahamic covenant, 11, 12, 85
acclamatio, 15
action and consequence, xiv–xv
"added to," 92
agency, human, xiv–xv, 26, 32, 75
Alexander, Samuel, 59
Alma the Younger
    on judgmental immediacy of thoughts and actions, xv
    on the seed of faith, 45–46
Aratus (Greek poet), 65
astronomy, xiii–xiv, xx
Atonement, of Jesus Christ
    access to, through suffering, xvi, xviii
    cleansing effect of, 4–5
    exalting power of, 63–64
    healing and reconciling power of, 16
    keynote of morning song of Creation, 15
Augustine, Saint, 68–69

B

Babylonian captivity, 5, 6–7
Ballard, M. Russell, 60
Beatitudes, the, 45
Beattie, Melodie, 79
Beck, Julie B., 46
Beecher, Henry Ward, 79
Bennion, Lowell C., 43
Bernard of Clairvaux, 80
big-picture understanding, xx, 4–10, 23, 54, 91

Blake, William, v, xi, 87
body, human
    death and rebirth of, 71
    fallen nature of, 14, 68, 85
    record written in, xiv–xv
Bonaparte, Napoleon, 70
brother of Jared, theophany of, 23
Browning, Robert, 75–76
"brown music," 29
Burtt, E. A., v
Busche, F. Enzio, 3–4
Bynum, Caroline Walker, 76–77n17

C

Catherine of Siena, xii, xix, xx, 46
charitable actions, 81, 84
childhood, optimism of, 1–3
Christmas, F. Enzio Busche's memory of, 3–4
"compound in one" (Lehi), xi, xvi, 74–75, 86
comprehension, limits of human, xii
consciousness, noncompetitive nature of human, 88–89
cosmos
    displays God's love, 24, 25, 40n3, 74, 80
    Greek term for, 40, 40n3
    harmony of, as mark of the divine, 15, 28–29, 32, 67, 74
    human co-ownership of, 81, 83, 85
    as mechanical clock, 1, 36, 70
    order of, according to Leibniz, 32–33
    sphere of action for God's saving work, 22, 26
creation, of earth
    bears record of God's love, xiii–xiv, 13, 24–25, 65, 74, 85
    details of world determined at time of, 30
    difference vs. sameness in, 31, 34–35, 36, 37–39
    and "endless variety," 34–35
    gratitude for, 89
    Jesus Christ's role in, 15, 19–20n8
    morning song of, 15
    not fully contingent on God, 32–33
    order and fecundity balanced at 29, 32, 39
    remembering Lord's mercy since, 13, 16
creative difference, 37, 39

D

death
    as cosmic ground state, 65–66
    essential for rebirth and resurrection, 71–72
    Jesus Christ's submission to, 52, 63, 72, 87

INDEX

Jesus Christ's victory over, xvi–xv, 62–63, 68, 72, 74
as release from mortal bondage, 60–61
sown in mortal body, 71
deism, 36
Descartes, René, 70
Dickinson, Emily, v, 86, 88

E

earth. *See also* creation, of earth
endless variety of, 29, 34–35
exploitation of, 81–83
fall of, xx, 28, 65, 68, 73
God created best possible version of, xiv, 26–28, 30–32
gratitude for, 89
human co-ownership of, xiv, 82–83
manifests God's love or existence, 24, 28, 40n3, 65, 74, 80
meek to inherit, 81
purpose of, xiv, 65
redemption and sanctification of, xiv
sentience of, 72–73
stewardship over, 82
"Easter in ordinary" (Lash), xx
Einstein, Albert, 75
Eliot, T. S., xiii, 67, 91
Enoch, grasps depth of God's love, 8, 23, 24
entitlement vs. stewardship mentality over earth's resources, 81–82
Epicureans, 65–66, 69–70, 73
eternal life, 22, 24, 64, 68, 82, 84, 85, 87, 92
evil
God not responsible for, 33
necessity of, xiv, 27, 28, 67
not evidence against God, 67–69
problem of, 66–67
in tension between order and fecundity, 33
turned to good end by God, 68

F

faith
necessity of, ix–x
seed of, 17, 45–46
Faust, James E., 50
fecundity. *See* order and fecundity
freedom
in Leibniz's universe, 30–31
of spirit upon death, 61
truth and, 59–60

G

Galileo, 25, 70
gathering. *See* Israel, gathering of
Gethsemane, 52

gifts of the Spirit, 44
God. *See also* love of God
    existence of, denied, 69, 70
    foreknowledge of, 30, 32
    mercy and patience of, xii, 17, 22
    peace of, xvii, 54, 55, 69
    weeps over sin, 27
    wisdom of, 54
Golgotha, 52
gospel
    affords wider vision, xx, 54
    assigns value to physical universe, v, 22
    blessings of, xvii, xviii, xix, 1, 2, 4, 14, 16, 47, 62
    encourages synergistic blend of human differences, 38, 43, 68
    grace-filled nature of, 48–49
    "happifying" message of, xvii–xix, 27, 52
    hard and easy nature of, 55, 67
    miracle of, xvi
    obedience to, 11, 16
    "scandal" of, 45
    sharing a feature of, economy, 25, 83
    stewardship enjoined by, 82–83
    teaches progressive return to God, xii
    unconditional happiness via, xvi, xix
grace, of God
    compensates for personal weakness, 53
    likened to vibrant bounce on gospel path, 46
    manifested in God's love, 24, 74
    mortal hardship relieved by, xvii
    recognizing, leads to sharing it with others, 48–49
    salvation by, 47
grapes, Galileo's analogy of, 25
gratitude, xix, 81, 89, 91, 92
Greatest Generation, 12
Greek atomists, 35

H

"happifying," xvi, xvii, 56n4
happiness
    bottom-up vs. top-down reckoning of, xix–xx
    a by-product, not a goal, 51, 52
    finding, 45, 50–53, 84
    mingling of, with pain, xvi
    mortality a foretaste of eternal, xi
    possible through Christ's victory over death, xvii, 68
    self-forgetfulness and, 44–45, 48
heaven. *See also* mortality: heavenlike nature of
    blessings of, on offer, xi, xii
    councils in, 15, 19–20n8
    declares glory of God, xiii, 2
    inspires upward reach, 75–76

INDEX

hell, xi, xii, xiv, 28
Hölderlin, Friedrich, xviii, 68
Holland, Jeffrey R., 15
Holy Ghost
    aids remembrance, 14
    impressions of, xv–xvi
    witness of, a foretaste of eternal salvation, 61–62
"Human Immortality" (James), 88
humility, 44, 47, 52, 53, 81, 83

I

individuals
    exist in interactive unity, 43–44
    value of, 32, 39
Industrial Revolution, 12
Isaiah
    illuminates God's overarching purposes, 7, 63
    Nephi and Jacob find solace in writings of, 6
    prophesies of Christ, 62–63, 87
Israel, gathering of, 6–7, 11, 57n4

J

Jacob (brother of Nephi), pines for ancestral homeland, 6
James, William, 81, 88–89
"Jesus, the Very Thought of Thee" (Clairvaux), 80

Jesus Christ. *See also* Atonement, of Jesus Christ
    descended below all things, 15, 16, 52, 63, 87
    devotion to, makes mortality heavenlike, xii, 62
    fellowship with, xvi
    God's love revealed through, 80
    Light of, 91
    as "man of sorrows," 62–63, 87
    as Mediator, 64
    meekness of, 52, 87
John the Revelator, 15, 27
"joy, fulness of," 61. *See also* happiness
Judgment, the, xiv–xv, 11, 47, 64

K

Keller, Helen, 90–91
Kepler, Johannes, 70
Kimball, Heber C., 73
King, Arthur Henry, 51
kingdoms, in heaven, 34
Korihor, 84
kósmos (Greek), 39

L

Laman and Lemuel
    actions of, fairly normal, 64
    myopia of, 9
    rebellion of, 7, 49

Laplace, Pierre-Simon, 70
Lehi, concern for family and posterity, 49
Leibniz, Gottfried Wilhelm
- on blending of faith and intellect, 36
- on diversity in Creation, 36
- on earth as best of all possible worlds, 26–28, 30, 32
- on evil, 33
- on love of God as foretaste of future felicity, v
- on order of universe, 32
- on preestablished harmony of world, 30
- on principles of order and fecundity, 29, 33, 39

Levinas, Emmanuel, ix, 87
Lewis, C. S., v, 38, 44, 48
love of God
- abundance of, 25, 74
- depth of, xvi, 15, 22, 24–25, 32, 74
- distills on each person, 13, 25, 79
- Enoch grasps, 23
- failure to grasp, xviii
- importance of remembering, 13–14
- long-suffering nature of, 12
- manifested in cosmos, 22, 23–25, 40n3, 74, 80
- Moroni asks readers to reflect on, 12–13
- nature's witness of, 24, 75
- Nephi grasps long arc of, 7–12
- prayerful remembrance of, 18
- revealed through Jesus Christ, 80
- structures mortal experience, x, 24
- synonymous with God's saving work, 21, 26

M

mathematical systems, analogy of, 30–31
matter, living nature of, 33, 37, 74
Maxwell, Neal A., 37, 52
McConkie, Bruce R., xv
mercy. *See* God: mercy and patience of
Millay, Edna St. Vincent, 59
Monadology (Leibniz), 33
Moore, Marianne, v
Moroni
- concern for others' salvation, 47–48
- does not despair, 17
- receives divine grace, 53
- tasted of God's redemptive love, 17
- urges remembrance of God's mercy, 13–14

mortality
- challenges of, xvi, 1, 14, 27–28, 60–61, 68, 71, 74, 75
- as foretaste of eternal happiness or misery, xi, 61–62

INDEX

heavenlike nature of, v, xii–xiii, xx, 23, 46, 62, 89, 92
infused with celestial resonance, xii, xiv, 24, 80
preparatory state of, xi, 62
as priceless gift, xix
release from bondage of, 60–61
as three-act play, 4
Moses, theophany of, 23, 26
Mosiah, sons of, 49
multiplication miracles, of Christ, 25, 92
multiverse, 89

N

narcissism, 9, 18, 19, 50, 68, 85
nature
attitude toward, 73–74
endless variety in, 34–35
full of divinity, 39
laws of, reconceptualized, 38
as promise of new life, 72
redemption of, 73–74
as witness of God, xiii, 64–69, 71, 74–75, 85
Nephi
gains prophetic view of God's purposes, 5–12
prays for generations unborn, 7, 10, 48
New Jerusalem, 27
new name given to faithful, 37–38
Newton, Isaac, 36, 70
Nibley, Hugh, 14–15, 23

Nicodemus, 51
novelty and spontaneity in best possible world, 31, 36

O

obedience, 11, 16
degrees of, written in human body, xv
empowers people to live righteously, 11, 16
leads to freedom, 60
"Ode: Intimations of Immortality" (Wordsworth), 2
Okazaki, Chieko N., v, xix
opposition, 27–28, 56, 67–68, 74
order and fecundity, 29, 33, 39

P

Packer, Boyd K., analogy of three-act play, 4
pain, xvi, 27, 28, 61, 62, 65, 71, 74, 75, 91. *See also* suffering
patience, xix
Paul
on all things held together by Atonement, 15
on being "one body in Christ," 43
on Christ's humiliation, 52
on gifts of the Spirit, 44
on joy and peace of God in this life, xvii, 1

Paul (*continued*)
    on life and nature as witnesses of God, 65–67, 69
    on prayerful attentiveness to daily needs, 55
    on the Resurrection, 71–72
    on "scandal" of the gospel, 45, 56n3
    on tasting the love of God, 79–80
    on wisdom of God, 54
    on witness of Holy Ghost as foretaste of heaven, 61–62
    on working out one's own salvation, 46
peace. *See* God: peace of
Peirce, Charles Sanders, 38–39
philosophy, useful despite limits, ix
pneuma (Greek), 51–52
Pratt, Orson, 59
prayer
    about truth of Book of Mormon, 13–14
    brings personal peace, 55
    example of Nephi and Moroni, 17, 48
    Laman and Lemuel's lack of faith in, 9
    Nephi's, leads to knowing God's love and purposes, 5, 7, 9, 12, 64
    process of, seen in Shakespearean sonnet, 17–18
    soul-expanding nature of, 9–10, 14
preestablished harmony (Leibniz), 30
premortality, 2, 4–5, 14–15
primordial revelation, doctrine of, 23
prophets, sweeping visions of, 8, 10, 23, 34

R

remembering, importance of, 13–14, 17, 18
repentance, xv, 5, 22, 32, 63, 68
Rescher, Nicholas, 30
resurrection, xvii, 61, 71–72
revelation
    personal, 8–9, 46, 52, 91
    primordial, 23
Rhodes, Cecil, 82
Roosevelt, Eleanor, 51, 52

S

sacrifice, xvii, xviii, xx
salvation
    anxious, self-centered quest for, 48–52, 55
    divine help in working out one's own, 46–47, 62
    grace the taproot of, 46
    Nephi and Moroni's concern for others', 47–48
    promise of, embodied in nature, 71–72, 75–76

INDEX

sameness
    arguments against, in nature's productions, 34–35, 39
    Isaac Newton gave priority to, 36
    reduction of nature's endless variety to, 35
    relationship of sin to, 37
Satan, xvi, 50–51, 53, 68, 86
science, older vs. modern view of reality, 35–36, 65–66, 70–71
seed, analogy of rebirth, 60, 64, 71–72, 76–77n17. *See also* faith: seed of
self-aggrandizement, 50
self-forgetfulness
    attribute of Christlike love, 52
    yields happiness, 44–45, 48
Sermon on the Mount, 45
Shakespeare, William, 17–18
Shaw, George Bernard, 28
Smith, George A., 73
Smith, Joseph
    on God's boundless mercies and blessings, 82
    on people's desire to bless human race, 48, 56n4
    on self-aggrandizement, 50
snowflakes, analogy of, 39
Stevens, Wallace, 86
stewardship, of earth, xiv, 73, 81–83, 89, 92
suffering
    assimilating, to that of Christ, xvi
    death a release from, xvii, 14, 27, 60–61, 63–64
    developing Christlike nature through, xvi–xvii, 45
    finding joy amid, xix, 46
    freedom from, 14, 27, 54, 56
    turned to good, xvi, xviii–xix, 7, 9, 16, 55, 61, 68, 87
Sullivan, Anne, 90

T

Taylor, John (Church president), xiv
Taylor, John F. A. (philosopher), x
testimony, bearing of, 15
Theodicy (Leibniz), 26
Thomas, Dylan, 68
Thoreau, Henry David, 1, 21, 39, 69, 79, 83, 93n7
thoughts, judgmental immediacy of, xv
Tolstoy, Leo, 22, 32, 51
tomato seeds, story of, 60
trials. *See* suffering

U

universe
    "editions" of, 88–89
    manifests God's love and majesty, 23, 84, 87

V

variety, in creation, 29, 34–35.
    See also creative
    difference
via dolorosa, 28

W

weakness, human, xvii, 69, 87,
    92
Wells, Daniel H., 73
Westfall, Richard, 35–36
Whitehead, Alfred North, 55–56
"white music," 29
white stone given to faithful,
    37–38
Williams, Thomas, funeral of,
    60
wisdom, of God, 24, 28, 54
Wittgenstein, Ludwig, 85
Wordsworth, William, 2, 91

Y

Young, Brigham, xiii, xiv, xviii,
    xix, 34, 37, 39, 56–57,
    60–61, 71, 73, 82

Z

Zion, 6, 24, 57, 73